給渴望展開新生活的你

尋找人生目標
的45種方法

作者ChatGPT・譯者ChatGPT・封面繪圖Shutterstock AI

全世界第一本ChatGPT全創作書籍！

　　這本書，是從「直接回應企劃者個人與社會大眾好奇心」的角度而策劃出來的。

　　「我們如何區分 AI 和實際作者撰寫的稿件？」

　　「我們可以收集資料並用自然語言來說服人嗎？」

　　「對於出版外國書籍來說，最重要的翻譯過程是否已經能夠完全用人工智能取代？」

　　「校對已經升級到不需要專業人員的地步了嗎？」

「我可以寫出比有專業知識的作家更好的文章嗎？」

「一本書要保持整體流暢是一項非常困難的工作。AI可能做得到嗎？」

「我真的能夠藉由AI設計出一個商業化的封面嗎？」

……之所以會先關注並去探討諸如此類的問題，是一種職業本能。

透過這次出版工作，我們對於最初產生的這些問題有了能去發展的各種答案與方向。而對個人來說，這也是一段可以去猜測未來商業發展可能的探索時期。

希望大家也能在這本《尋找人生目標的45種方法》中找到回應自己好奇心的答案。

關於本書的10個事實

1. 本書的書名和各章節主題不是由 AI 所創建的。為了觀察編輯人員與 ChatGPT AI 之間的合作，我們從出版社正在保留或尚未推出的計劃中選出書稿。

2. 目錄大綱是用英文提出的，各項問題的內容則已在正文中提供。

3. 為了便於比較中文譯稿和英文原稿，所以全書以中英對照的方式呈現。

4. 我們所下的指令需求是每次產生大約5,000個字，但AI生成的原稿卻不超過3,000個字。由於產生更多文字的

文本生成權限受到限制，我們未能找到使用方法。

5. 韓文版所有英文都是透過Naver Papago翻譯成韓文，並由一名多益(TOEIC)成績約900分的工作人員進行簡單的審查。中文版則是由ChatGPT將英文翻譯成中文，並由一名托福(TOEFL)約110分的工作人員進行審查。

6. 封面製作使用了多種對公眾開放的平台，並且多次反覆要求更好的設計。目前的封面設計是在對Shutterstock AI提供了書名、目錄、主題以及對應原始內容的表達技巧之後所得到的，但最終封面則是由企劃編輯選擇出來的。由於無法透過免費模式獲得高品質的設計，所以還是轉換並採用付費模式，在使用上依然受到限制。

不過，在改變表達技巧並對同樣主題添加一些詞語的過程中，AI已清楚展示出自己的進化。現有封面就是AI自行理解所提供書名之後的結果。

7. 編輯人員檢視了整份文稿，並且只進行有限的校對以對應讀者需求。

8. 針對譯稿混合了口語表達與寫作方式的部分,全文已統一成書寫風格的形式。

9. 文中刪除了許多逗號、引號和刪節號,因為它們被大量過度使用在連接詞之後或較難理解的句子裡;同時也刪除了部分不必要的內容,以求提高文章通順度。

10. 不含印刷製程,韓文版原書稿總共花費30小時,由2名編輯工作人員完成。而印製裝訂等過程則總共花費7天,直到首次面市銷售。至於中文版書稿則總共花費150小時,亦由2名編輯人員完成。從印刷裝訂到通路上架出版,亦為7天。

　　人生是一段充滿波折的旅程，看不到清晰的終點何在。常常我們發現自己迷失其中、不斷尋找目標和意義，所幸能去探索的路徑很多，而且無論什麼時候開始都不嫌遲。在這本書中，我們將探討 45 種找出人生目標的方法，從永恆不變的世間真理，到重要人際關係與感情，這種種事物，就讓我們一起啟程去追尋。

第一章：建立真正的關係

　　人與人的「關係」可說是實踐人生目標的重要本源。這個篇章將探究我們與家人、朋友、愛人之間培養感情的重要性，同時，也將探討社區參與、主動與他人展開深刻連結所能帶來的益處。

第二章：找到人生中的滿足感

　　知道自己想要什麼以及怎麼去定義衡量所謂的成功，是找到人生目標的關鍵。在這一章，我們將談到設定明確目標與建構達標準則的重要性，也將探究如何在實踐目標與滿足現狀之間找到理想的平衡。

第三章：讓自己開心度過每一天

　　說到追求人生目標與幸福，往往生活中的微小事物卻能造成極大影響。在這一章，我們將挖掘如何讓那些能帶來喜悅與滿足的深刻小事填滿我們的生活，並分享正念與感謝的益處，以及如何將它們帶入我們的日常之中。

第四章：接受人生中不變的真理

　　置身在這個不斷變動的世界，我們很容易對真正重要的事物視而不見。在這一章，我們將探討人們世代以來始終奉為圭臬的不變真理，例如誠實、正直，以及善良慈悲。這些價值觀正是人生的基礎，為我們充滿高低起伏的生命路途提供可以依循的道德羅盤。

第五章：覺察人生目標的根基所在

　　每個人的人生目標各有起因。有些人會在他們的職涯或事業中找到意義，有些人則會在他們的人際關係、興趣

嗜好、或是靈性追求中得到感應。在這個章節裡，我們將探究不同目標的根基起源，以及該怎麼覺察自己的人生目標從何而來。

第六章：讓情緒成為成功的助力

　　情感是一種強大的力量，在追求人生目標的過程中，它可以是助力，也可能是阻礙。在這一章中，我們將談到如何以正向的方式來運用情感、為成功添加動能，並探討高情商帶來的好處，以及如何讓它幫助我們實現更加優越的個人與專業成就。

　　尋找人生目標是一場不斷前進的旅程，需要耐心、自我省視，以及一種願意去探索不同可能性的意志。透過擁抱指引我們的永恆真理、找出人生目標來源，設定自我滿意標準、培養美好人際關係、明智運用情感，並且快樂度過每一天，我們就能創造出充滿意義的生活。現在就勇往直前，讓我們一起去找出人生目標吧！

| Prologue |

Life is a journey full of twists and turns, with no clear destination in sight. Often, we find ourselves lost and searching for purpose and meaning in our lives. The good news is that there are many paths to discover our purpose, and it's never too late to start. In this book, we will explore 45 ways to find a purpose in life, covering everything from the timeless truths that never change to the importance of relationships and emotions. Let's begin the journey together.

Chapter 1: The Importance of Precious Relationships

Our relationships with others can be a major source of purpose and fulfillment in life. In this chapter, we'll explore the importance of nurturing our relationships with family, friends, and romantic partners. We'll also discuss the benefits of community involvement and volunteering to create meaningful connections with others.

Chapter 2: What criteria and how will you be satisfied?

Knowing what you want and how you'll measure your success is crucial for finding purpose. In this chapter, we'll discuss the importance of setting goals and establishing criteria for satisfaction. We'll explore how to find the right balance between achieving our goals and being content with what we have.

Chapter 3: Fill the Day Happily

The little things in life can make a big difference when it comes to finding purpose and happiness. In this chapter, we'll explore how to fill our days with small but meaningful activities that bring joy and fulfillment. We'll discuss the benefits of mindfulness and gratitude, and how to incorporate them into our daily lives.

Chapter 4: Truth that does not change in life

In a world of constant change, it's easy to lose sight of the things that truly matter. In this chapter, we'll explore the timeless truths that have guided people for generations, such as honesty, integrity, and compassion. These values serve as a foundation for a purposeful life, providing a moral compass to navigate through the ups and downs of life.

Chapter 5: Where is your sense of purpose based?

The source of our purpose can be different for everyone.

Some find their sense of purpose in their career or vocation, while others find it in their relationships, hobbies, or spirituality. In this chapter, we'll explore the various sources of purpose and how to identify where your sense of purpose comes from.

Chapter 6: How to Use Emotions in a Way That Helps Success

Emotions are a powerful force that can either hinder or help us in our quest for purpose. In this chapter, we'll explore how to use our emotions in a positive way to fuel our success. We'll discuss the benefits of emotional intelligence and how to develop it for greater personal and professional success.

Finding purpose in life is an ongoing journey, one that requires patience, self-reflection, and a willingness to explore new possibilities. By embracing the timeless truths that guide us, identifying the source of our purpose, setting criteria for satisfaction, nurturing our relationships, using our emotions wisely, and filling our days with happiness, we can create a purposeful and fulfilling life. Let's go forth and discover our purpose together.

| 目 次 |

Chpater 1.
建立真正的關係

此圖為AI以書名、目錄和主題為指令而繪製的封面初稿之一。

第一章聚焦在一個重要課題，就是我們能從哪裡感受到人生意義，尤其是指我們與他人之間的關係。那些圍繞在我們身邊的人，不但會深刻影響我們對人生目標與滿足感的認知，也能讓我們對如何培養健康而深具意義的關係有更多的了解。

　　而在這章中首先要談的，就是千萬不要草率建立關係。也就是說，在完全投入一段關係之前，必須好好花時間了解對方；同時也要留意，一旦跟那些可能不符合我們價值觀與目標的人建立關係之後，所將帶來的潛在後果。

　　接著要探討的，則是關係的切割。要知道，並不是所有關係都是平等的，所以去按照對我們的重要性來優先考慮某些關係，其實是沒有問題的。也唯有藉由切割關係並專注在那些真正要緊的人身上，我們才能跟他們建立更深入、更有意義的連結。

本章也強調，把精力花在建立並維繫健康的關係，是一件非常重要的事。因為當我們投入於人際關係的經營，不僅加強了與那個人的連結，而且也增進了我們對於人生目標與自我滿足的覺察。所以必須知道，真正的關係需要努力，美好的關係更需要時間去建立。

　　另一方面，這一章也提出警告，就是千萬不要僅僅為了利益而去建立關係。儘管尋求對我們有益的關係可能很誘人，但這種方式只會導致膚淺、無法令人滿足的交際，最終並不能為我們追求人生目標有什麼幫助。

　　同時，本章也告訴我們，並不是所有的關係都是正向或有益的。不可避免地，我們總會遇到把痛苦和負能量帶進生命中的人，但大家要記住，就算是負面經驗，也能夠提供寶貴的教訓以及成長的機會。

　　最後，這一章還強調一定要跟真誠可信的人好好交往。如果我們身邊都是價值觀與目標一致的人，那麼就能建立起更深刻而有意義的關係，並對我們追求人生目標有所助益。

　　總歸來說，針對建立有意義的人際關係以尋得人生目

標，本書第一章提出寶貴的見解與忠告。藉由明確認知花時間去建構關係的重要性、排出真正重要的優先順序、投入在健康的關係上、避開只為好處而產生的關係、從負面經驗中學習、並且找出真誠實在的交誼，那麼，我們才能建立起基礎強大的關係，進而讓生命中的目標得以實現。

Chapter 1 focuses on the important topic of where our sense of purpose in life is based, specifically in relation to our relationships with others. This chapter explores the idea that the people we surround ourselves with can greatly impact our sense of purpose and fulfillment, and offers advice on how to cultivate healthy and meaningful relationships.

The first topic discussed in this chapter is the importance of not making relationships recklessly. This means taking the time to get to know someone before fully investing in a relationship, and being mindful of the potential consequences of forming a relationship with someone who may not align with our value sand goals.

The next topic covered is the idea of separating relationships. It's important to recognize that not all relationships are
created equal, and it's okay to prioritize certain relationships
over others based on their significance in our lives. By separating relationships and focusing on those that truly matter,
we can build deeper and more meaningful connections with
the people who matter most to us.

The chapter also highlights the importance of putting
effort into building and maintaining healthy relationships.
When we invest in our relationships, we not only strengthen
the bond with that person but also improve our own sense of
purpose and fulfillment. It's important to recognize that true
relationships require effort and that good relationships take
time to build.

On the other hand, the chapter also cautions against
forming relationships solely for the sake of usefulness. While
it may be tempting to seek out relationships that can benefit
us in some way, this approach can lead to shallow and
unfulfilling connections that ultimately do not contribute to our
sense of purpose in life.

The chapter also acknowledges that not all relationships will be positive or beneficial. Inevitably, we will encounter people who bring pain and negativity into our lives. However, the chapter encourages readers to remember that even negative experiences can provide valuable lessons and opportunities for growth.

Finally, the chapter emphasizes the importance of investing in relationships with people who are true and authentic. By surrounding ourselves with people who align with our values and goals, we can build deeper and more meaningful connections that contribute to our sense of purpose in life.

In conclusion, Chapter 1 of your book provides valuable insights and advice on building healthy and meaningful relationships that can contribute to our sense of purpose in life. By recognizing the importance of taking time to form relationships, prioritizing those that truly matter, investing in healthy relationships, avoiding relationships based solely on usefulness, learning from negative experiences, and seeking out authentic connections, readers can build a strong foundation of relationships that support their purpose and fulfillment in life.

01

避免建立輕率的關係

··

　　輕率與人建立關係，會成為人生目標的阻礙。而所謂
「輕率的關係」，指的就是不良的、或在某些方面會造成
傷害的各種關係，無論來自這個人的行為，這個關係的本
質，或是其他因素。

　　這些型態的關係，會讓你極度心神不寧，無法專注在
自己與所追求的目標上。包括那些總讓你失望、造成你陰
影的人，對你過度控制、需索無度的人，或是耗盡你所有
時間、精力去對應的人，若不顧後果與他們維持往來，將
嚴重阻礙你對人生目標的追尋。

而輕率關係最棘手的地方，就是難以辨識。因為在一段新的關係裡，我們很容易被刺激感與驚喜感所吸引，以至於沒有注意到它在生活中所帶來的負面影響。你可能意識到自己在為這些人的行為找藉口，或完全忽視自己的需要與渴望，只為了想博得他們的好感。

想避免輕率的關係，第一步就是要能對這類徵兆有所警覺。**如果你經常覺得不快樂、感到有壓力，或者身邊有人總是耗盡你的心力、控制你的生活，那大概就是到了該重新檢視這段關係的時候了。**另外一些警訊則包括：跟他人相處時經常覺得自己如履薄冰、覺得不能做自己，或是總是感到自己的付出遠比得到的多。

如果你發現自己確實已深陷於輕率的關係，下一步就要採取行動。意思是你可能需要針對關係中的問題，有技巧地跟對方開啟對話；也可能意味著必須全然終止這段關係。儘管要放手讓在乎的人走會很難，但千萬要記住，你自己的快樂與幸福才是最重要的。

一旦從輕率的關係中解脫，你將發現自己擁有更多時間、能量以及好情緒，去致力於你的目標與熱情所在。這對於追求人生意義來說是決定性的一步，因為它讓你得以

專注在自己以及所需要的事物上面，而不是一直被不愉快的、充滿傷害的關係所糾纏。

　　的確，避免輕率的關係並不容易。因為我們都是人，也都會犯錯。但如果能對這類不良關係的徵兆有所警覺，並在必要時願意去採取行動，那就可以在尋求人生目標時躲掉大這個大障礙。請務必記得，**你值得快樂、健康、滿足，而輕率的關係不太可能幫助你實現這些目標**。所以，如果你發現置身於一段對自己無益的關係中，那麼現在也許正是**轉身離開、把焦點放在自己身上**的時候。

Having a reckless relationship with anyone can be a serious hindrance to finding a purpose in life. When we say "reckless relationship", we're talking about relationships that are unhealthy or harmful in some way, whether it's due to the partner's behavior, the nature of the relationship itself, or other factors.

These types of relationships can be incredibly distracting, and they can keep you from focusing on yourself and your goals. Whether it's a toxic partner who brings you down, a partner who is overly controlling or demanding, or simply a relationship that takes up all of your time and energy, a reckless relationship can be a major obstacle to finding your purpose in life.

One of the biggest challenges with reckless relationships is that they can be hard to identify. It's easy to get caught up in the drama and excitement of a new relationship, and not notice the negative effects it's having on your life. You might find yourself making excuses for your partner's behavior, or ignoring your own needs and desires in order to please them.

The first step in avoiding a reckless relationship is to be aware of the signs. If you find yourself constantly unhappy or stressed out, or if your partner is always demanding your attention or controlling your life, it may be time to re-evaluate the relationship. Other warning signs might include feeling like you're constantly walking on eggshells around your partner, feeling like you can't be yourself, or feeling like you're always giving more than you're getting.

If you do find yourself in a reckless relationship, the next step is to take action. This might mean having a difficult conversation with your partner about the problems in the relationship, or it might mean ending the relationship altogether. It can be hard to let go of someone you care about, but it's important to remember that your own happiness and well-being should always come first.

Once you've freed yourself from a reckless relationship, you'll likely find that you have more time, energy, and emotional resources to devote to your own goals and passions. This is a crucial step in finding your purpose in life, as it allows you to focus on yourself and your own needs, rather than being constantly distracted by a toxic or harmful relationship.

Of course, avoiding a reckless relationship isn't always easy. We're all human, and we all make mistakes. But by being aware of the signs of a toxic relationship, and by being willing to take action when necessary, you can avoid one of the biggest obstacles to finding your purpose in life. Remember, you deserve to be happy, healthy, and fulfilled, and a reckless relationship is unlikely to help you achieve those goals. So if you find yourself in a relationship that isn't serving your best interests, it may be time to move on and focus on yourself.

02

學會切割無關緊要的關係

學著去分辨出哪些人只是路過，會是探尋人生目標過程中很困難但卻有必要的一個部分。在一生中，我們很自然地會跟不計其數的人產生關聯。其中有些關係深刻、充滿意義，有些卻很偶然、極其短暫。但我們總想牢牢抓住所有關係，即便是不經意的交往也不放掉。而這樣就會使得我們很難真實活在當下，也沒有辦法去追求我們真正的目標與熱情所在。

那麼，究竟「分辨出哪些人只是路過」是什麼意思？其實就是指對於已經走到盡頭、不再對我們有益處的關係，要能夠看得出來。我們可能得去結束一段不再令人滿

足的友誼或戀情，也有可能要讓自己疏遠那些負面、惡毒的人。

想要能夠辨別短暫的人際關係，我們需要在一件事情上對自己誠實，那就是「與他人交往，我們真正渴望或需求的是什麼」。這意味著我們願意捨棄那些不再對自己有益的關係，即便再困難、再痛苦也願意放手；這也代表著我們願意去對那些負面、有害的人設定界線，並把時間與精力放在真正有用、能夠滿足我們的關係上。

專注於跟真正要緊的人進行深入而有意義的交往，是脫離短暫關係的一個方法。也就是說，**我們必須投入時間與精力在最重要的關係上，在跟這些人相處時，要認真用心。**同時，這也代表著我們會斷開那些不再讓人滿足的交際，而去尋找與我們價值觀及人生目標一致的新關係。

參與活動、去追求與我們興趣和熱情相符的事物，是與短暫關係切割的另一個方法。這可能包括尋找新的嗜好與興趣，或對發展事業及個人目標展開行動。**藉由專注於真正重要的事物，我們就能把志趣相投的人吸引到生活裡來，並與他們建立更加深刻、更有意義的關係。**

而擺脫短暫關係，也意味著能夠去原諒，並且能從過往的衝突與負面經驗中再出發前行。這表示我們能放下恩怨，聚焦在人際關係的積極面向上。也代表著為了建立更強大重要的關係，我們願意坦誠溝通，並對我們所在乎的人誠實。

　　總之，與短暫的關係切割是尋找人生目標過程中困難卻必要的一環。這需要我們在「與他人交往的真正渴望和需求」上對自己誠實，並願意放下令人不滿的關係。透過專注於跟真正對我們重要的人建立深厚、有意義的情誼，以及追求符合我們真正興趣與熱情的活動和嗜好，我們才能在生活中創造出對於目標與滿足的覺知。

Separating the relationships that are passing by can be a difficult but necessary part of finding purpose and meaning in life. As we go through life, we naturally form connections with a wide range of people. Some of these connections are deep and meaningful, while others are more casual and passing. While it can be tempting to hold onto all of our relationships, even the passing ones, doing so can prevent us from truly living in the present and pursuing our true goals and passions.

So, what does it mean to separate the relationships that are passing by? It means recognizing when a relationship has run its course and is no longer serving our best interests. This may involve letting go of friendships or romantic relationships that are no longer fulfilling, or distancing ourselves from people who are negative or toxic.

Separating the relationships that are passing by requires us to be honest with ourselves about what we truly want and need from our connections with others. It means being willing to let go of relationships that are no longer serving our best interests, even if it is difficult or painful to do so. It also means being willing to set boundaries with people who are negative or toxic, and to focus our time and energy on the relationships that are truly meaningful and fulfilling.

One way to separate the relationships that are passing by is to focus on building deep and meaningful connections with the people who truly matter to us. This means investing time and effort into the relationships that are most important, and being present and attentive when we are with those individuals. It also means being willing to let go of relationships that are no longer fulfilling, and to seek out new connections that are in line with our values and goals.

Another way to separate the relationships that are passing by is to engage in activities and pursuits that are in line with our true interests and passions. This may involve pursuing new hobbies or interests, or taking steps to advance our careers or personal goals. By focusing on the things that truly matter to us, we can attract like-minded people into our lives and build deeper, more meaningful connections with them.

Separating the relationships that are passing by can also

involve being willing to forgive and move on from past conflicts or negative experiences. This means being willing to let go of grudges and resentments, and focusing on the positive aspects of our relationships. It also means being willing to communicate openly and honestly with those we care about, in order to build stronger and more meaningful connections with them.

In conclusion, separating the relationships that are passing by can be a difficult but necessary part of finding purpose and meaning in life. It involves being honest with ourselves about what we truly want and need from our connections with others, and being willing to let go of relationships that are no longer fulfilling. By focusing on building deep and meaningful connections with the people who truly matter to us, and pursuing the activities and pursuits that are in line with our true interests and passions, we can create a sense of purpose and fulfillment in our lives.

03

好的關係，
需要花費心力去建立

建立並維繫良好的關係，要靠時間、努力與奉獻。這需要一種可以用來向對方展現、並讓自己盡責以保持關係穩固的承諾。而只要提到真正的關係，也就是那些建立在以誠實、尊重、信任為基礎的人際往來，這樣的承諾就特別重要。

有效的溝通是所有良好關係的核心。這代表著願意傾聽，分享自己的想法與感受，並且用一種尊重且具建設性的方式來解決任何歧見。這也表示對其他人抱持開放與坦誠的態度，即便這樣做會很困難、很彆扭。

建立良好關係的另一個關鍵，就是展現同理心與同情心。意思就是要把自己放在對方的位置上，試著去了解他們的觀點，而且就算情況再糟，也要給予支持和關懷。這也意味著願意妥協、為對方犧牲，但不會因此而放棄自己的需要或底限。

也正因為要建構並維繫良好的關係，所以耐心與理解也很重要。人際關係從來都不容易，就像路上總會有各種顛簸隨行。如果可以對他人保持耐性，並且認知到他們可能正在跟自己的挑戰與掙扎搏鬥，那麼就能向建立起強勁持久的關係大步邁進。

當然，**建立良好關係是一條雙向路，雙方都需要做出承諾好讓關係運作，並且必須投入必要的時間與努力來讓情況維持完好。**這代表著願意妥協，有效溝通，以及解決可能引發的任何問題。

而當探討到真正的關係，也就是那些建構在誠實、尊重、與信任之上的人際交往時，投入也就更高。因為這些關係通常是我們生命中最重要的，所以需要更深層的承諾與奉獻。但當雙方都願意為此而努力，那麼所得到的回報也將不可估量。

終歸來說，良好關係的建立與維持，攸關為對方挺身而出，願意解決挑戰與困難，並且投入必要的努力以保持關係的堅實。而且無論是愛人關係、朋友關係、還是家庭關係，這些原則都適用。當雙方都願致力要讓關係實現，那麼，所將獲得的成長、幸福、與滿足，也將無可限量。

Building and maintaining a good relationship takes time, effort, and dedication. It requires a commitment to showing up for the other person and doing your part to keep the relationship strong. When it comes to true relationships, those that are built on a foundation of honesty, respect, and trust, this commitment is especially important.

At the heart of any good relationship is effective communication. This means being willing to listen, share your own thoughts and feelings, and work through any disagreements in a respectful and constructive way. It also means being open and honest with the other person, even when it might be difficult or uncomfortable to do so.

Another key aspect of building a good relationship is showing empathy and compassion for the other person. This means putting yourself in their shoes, trying to understand their perspective, and being supportive and caring, even when things get tough. It also means being willing to compromise and make sacrifices for the other person, without sacrificing your own needs or boundaries.

In order to build and maintain a good relationship, it's also important to be patient and understanding. Relationships aren't always easy, and there are likely to be bumps in the road along the way. Being patient with the other person, and recognizing that they may be dealing with their own challenges and struggles, can go a long way towards building a strong and lasting connection.

Of course, building a good relationship is a two-way street. Both parties need to be committed to making the relationship work, and putting in the time and effort necessary to keep things strong. This means being willing to compromise, communicate effectively, and work through any issues that may arise.

When it comes to true relationships, those that are built on a foundation of honesty, respect, and trust, the stakes are even higher. These relationships are often the most important ones in our lives, and they require a deep level of commitment and dedication. But when both parties are willing to put in the work, the rewards can be immeasurable.

Ultimately, building and maintaining a good relationship is about showing up for the other person, being willing to work through challenges and difficulties, and putting in the effort necessary to keep the connection strong. Whether it's a romantic relationship, a friendship, or a family relationship, these principles apply. And when both parties are committed to making the relationship work, the possibilities for growth, happiness, and fulfillment are truly limitless.

關係太多，
反而無法擁有真正的關係

在通訊交流遠比從前更快速也更簡單的今日世界，很容易掉入交際膚淺的陷阱。我們在社交軟體上有數不清的朋友，但在真實生活中卻經常缺乏深度而有意義的連結。結果就是造成疏離感，寂寞孤單，並且缺乏人生目標。

事實上，建構一段好的關係需要付出時間、努力以及承諾。也就是必須投注於對方身上，為他們挺身而出，並在需要的時候陪在他們身邊。如果用一種散漫的態度去結交朋友，沒有付出必要的時間與努力，就不太可能會得到那種能夠幫助你成長、學習、找到人生目標的情誼。

溝通是建立美好關係的一個重要關鍵因素。在工作上，你需要做到對其他人開誠佈公，去傾聽他們想說什麼，還要能夠分享你的所知所感。也就是說，你要能展現脆弱，承認自己錯了，並且敞開心胸去面對所有反饋意見以及具建設性的批評。

　　另一個重要因素則是信任。因為**如果沒有信任，就無法建立穩固美好的關係。而這個信任指的就是要可靠、守承諾，並對他人誠實。同時也代表著就算事情不如預期，我們也願意去原諒別人，並接受自己被原諒。**

　　美好的人際交往也需要努力與承諾，所以要能投入必需的時間跟精力在建立關係上。意思是就算有生活中有種種其他事物出現，也要能把關係的經營排在優先。

　　如果用一種漫不經心的方式來面對人際關係，沒有付出必要的時間、努力，也不做任何承諾，就會很難得到好緣份。你可能空有一大堆認識的人，但卻缺乏深刻、有用的關係來幫助你達成人生目標。

　　終歸，建立良好關係的關鍵，在於要在意對方並且刻意經營。也就是願意投入於他人身上、出現他們眼前、聽

他們說話，並在他們需要的時候給予支持。同時，在必要時，也要能做出犧牲與妥協，以保持關係的穩固。

　　最後要提醒的是，我們生活中最重要的關係，就是那些建立於信任、溝通、努力與承諾之上的情誼。而這些也就是能夠幫助你成長、學習、找到人生目標的關係，也正是你值得投入之所在，無論要花多少時間與努力，都在所不惜。

In today's world, where communication is faster and easier than ever before, it's all too easy to fall into the trap of making superficial relationships. We have countless friends on social media, but often lack deep, meaningful connections in real life. The result is a sense of disconnection, loneliness, and a lack of purpose.

The truth is that building a good relationship takes time, effort, and commitment. It means being willing to invest in the other person, to show up for them and to be there for them when they need you. When you make a relationship in a loose way, without putting in the necessary time and effort, you are unlikely to meet a useful relationship that can help you grow, learn and find your purpose in life.

One of the key factors in building a meaningful relation-ship is communication. To make a relationship work, you need to be willing to talk openly and honestly with the other person, to listen to what they have to say, and to share your own thoughts and feelings. This means being willing to be vulnerable, to admit when you're wrong, and to be open to feedback and constructive criticism.

Another important factor is trust. Without trust, it's impossible to build a strong and meaningful relationship. This means being reliable, keeping your promises, and being honest with the other person. It also means being willing to forgive and to be forgiven, even when things don't go as planned.

A good relationship also requires effort and commitment. This means being willing to put in the time and energy necessary to build the relationship. It means being willing to prioritize the relationship, even when other things in your life get in the way.

When you make a relationship in a loose way, without putting in the necessary time, effort, and commitment, you are unlikely to meet a useful relationship. You may have plenty of acquaintances, but you'll lack the deep, meaningful connections that can help you find your purpose in life.

Ultimately, the key to building a good relationship is to be present and to be intentional. This means being willing to invest in the other person, to show up for them, to listen to them, and to be there for them when they need you. It also means being willing to make sacrifices and to compromise, when necessary, to keep the relationship strong.

In the end, the relationships that matter most in life are the ones that are built on a foundation of trust, communication, effort, and commitment. These are the relationships that can help you grow, learn, and find your purpose in life. And they are the ones that are worth investing in, even when it takes time and effort.

05

糟糕的關係，只會讓自己受苦

人是社交的動物，透過溝通與交流繁衍興盛。也唯有生活中的各種關係穩固健康，我們才能感到更加滿足，更有活力，也更具目標。相反的，要是遇人不淑，總是缺乏溝通、沒有信任、不被理解，我們的一生就會大大受苦。

這些糟糕關係帶來的最大問題之一，就是常會讓我們感到被孤立、很寂寞。即便被人群包圍，我們還是感覺不到跟他們有任何富意義的連結。我們也會有找不到人生方向的感覺，並可能苦苦掙扎於無法找到動機去追求目標與理想。

另一個問題則是這些糟糕的關係會讓人疲憊不堪、充滿壓力。當經常性地處於應付衝突、被人誤解、以及缺乏信任的關係之中，就會在身體或心理上付出代價。我們可能會感到焦慮、沮喪，或不知所措；也可能會為了要在生活中找到快樂與滿足而活得很辛苦。

　　為了避免這些負面影響，我們就要做到專注於建立健康而有意義的人際關係。也就是要去在意那些圍繞在我們身邊的人，並且願意投注必要的時間與努力，以建立穩固持久的關係。

　　建構健全關係的關鍵要素之一，就是溝通。如果可以跟生活周遭的人有效溝通，我們就比較能夠了解他們的需要、他們的企圖，以及他們的想法；也可以用一種具有建設性的方式來處理衝突與歧見；並將隨著時間去建立起彼此的信任與理解。

　　還有一個對建立良好關係很重要的元素，那就是同理心。**當我們能把自己放在他人的位置上，去了解他們所經歷過的事物與感受，也就比較能跟對方建立起連結。**我們越能展現出支持與關懷，也就越能幫助他們度過難關。

最後，如果能夠有意識地去選擇讓哪些人進入生活，就能避免爛關係的發生。**我們應該要投注必需的時間與努力去建立健康、有意義的連結，也要能夠放棄那些對我們來說沒有正面作用的關係。**

　　藉由建構起健康、有意義的關係，我們可以在生活中找到目標和滿足感，能讓自己身邊都被支持和激勵我們的人包圍，並且共同努力去實現目標和理想。我們也可以避開那些因為遇到糟糕的人而帶來的負面影響，例如覺得被孤立、充滿壓力，甚至找不到人生意義。

Human beings are social creatures, and we thrive on connection and community. When we have strong, healthy relationships in our lives, we feel more fulfilled, more energized, and more purposeful. But when we meet only clumsy relationships, those that are marked by a lack of connection, trust, and understanding, our lives can suffer greatly.

One of the biggest problems with clumsy relationships is that they often leave us feeling isolated and alone. We may be surrounded by people, but we don't feel connected to them in any meaningful way. We may lack a sense of purpose or direction in our lives, and we may struggle to find the motivation to pursue our goals and dreams.

Another problem with clumsy relationships is that they can be draining and stressful. When we're constantly dealing with conflict, misunderstandings, and a lack of trust in our relationships, it can take a toll on our physical and mental health. We may feel anxious, depressed, or overwhelmed, and we may struggle to find joy or fulfillment in our daily lives.

In order to avoid these negative consequences, it's important to focus on building healthy, meaningful relationships in our lives. This means being intentional about the people we surround ourselves with, and being willing to invest the time and effort necessary to build strong, lasting connections.

One of the key elements of a healthy relationship is communication. When we communicate effectively with the people in our lives, we're better able to understand their needs, their desires, and their perspectives. We're able to work through conflict and disagreements in a constructive way, and we're able to build trust and understanding over time.

Another important element of a healthy relationship is empathy. When we're able to put ourselves in the shoes of another person, to understand their experiences and their emotions, we're better able to build a connection with them. We're more likely to be supportive and caring, and we're more likely to be able to help them through difficult times.

Ultimately, the key to avoiding clumsy relationships is to be intentional about the people we let into our lives. We should be willing to invest the time and effort necessary to build healthy, meaningful connections, and to be willing to let go of relationships that aren't serving us in a positive way.

By building healthy, meaningful relationships, we can find purpose and fulfillment in our lives. We can surround ourselves with people who support and inspire us, and we can work together to achieve our goals and dreams. And we can avoid the negative consequences that come from meeting only clumsy relationships, such as isolation, stress, and a lack of purpose.

06

只要少數幾個人，
就能滿足真正需要的關係

與他人建立關係是人生中最重要的事情之一。因為人際關係能提供我們對於歸屬感、愛，以及有目標的感覺。但是我們可能認識很多人、交情很一般，卻只有極少數真正重要的人存在於生活之中。而他們就是支持我們、挑戰我們，並啟發我們讓自己做到最好的那些人。

關於「只要少數幾個人，就能滿足我們真正所需」的這個想法並不新。事實上，多年來已有許多哲學家、作家、思想家探討過這個概念。在《愛的藝術》一書中，埃里希·佛洛姆指出「通往真愛的唯一路徑就是要能與另一

個人建立起一種深刻而有意義的連結」。他也提到「愛不是感覺幸福，而是願意去犧牲」。

生命中最要緊的人，往往正是那些我們願意為他們犧牲的人。就算必須放棄自己所想、所要的一切，我們也會為了他們去做任何事。而這些人可能是我們的家人、摯友，或是愛人。

雖然對我們來說，真正重要的人可能很少，但這些人對我們人生所能造成的影響卻很大。因為他們是能幫助我們找到目標的人。他們能給予我們所需要的支持與鼓勵，讓我們能去追求目標與理想。他們能挑戰我們去成為最好的自己，讓我們極盡所能發揮潛力。他們還能啟發我們，讓我們更有同情心、更具同理心，並且更加有愛。

為了能真正感謝生命中最重要的人，我們就必須花時間去耕耘及培養與他們的關係。當與他們同在，我們要能表現出參與感與專注感，積極去傾聽他們想說什麼，也要透過行為和言詞去讓對方知道自己很在乎。同時，也要能夠去原諒，並在挑戰或衝突出現時，願意去解決。

當我們與生命中最重要的人建立穩固而有意義的連結

時，我們就更能感到充實、具有目標。因為這些關係可以讓我們有歸屬感，並且覺得自己可以對這個世界帶來好的改變。同時，他們還能給予我們喜悅與幸福的感受，而這些都是很難在生活中其他地方找到的。

當然，要知道這樣的關係並不是單向的。為了能真正從生活中最重要的人身上獲益，我們要能夠願意給予並懂得接受。當對方需要時，我們也要能挺身而出，給予他們支持與鼓勵，盡力讓自己成為他們生命中的正向影響。

總之，「只要少數幾個人，就能滿足我們真正所需」的這個概念很強大。雖然我們可能相交滿天下，但只有那些跟我們關係深厚的人才真的重要。而他們就是那些能為我們帶來目標、滿足感還有快樂的人。也唯有花時間去經營跟這些人的關係，我們才能針對生命中最重要的人表達感謝，並在這個世界中找到人生目標的更大意義。

One of the most important things in life is the relationships we form with others. These relationships can provide us with a sense of belonging, love, and purpose. While we may have many acquaintances and casual friendships, there are only a few people in our lives who really matter. These people are the ones who support us, challenge us, and inspire us to be our best selves.

The idea that only a few people are enough to really need is not a new one. In fact, it is a concept that has been explored by many philosophers, writers, and thinkers over the years. In his book, "The Art of Loving," Erich Fromm argues that "the only way to truly love is to be able to form a deep and meaningful connection with another person." He goes on to say that "love is not a feeling of happiness. Love is a willingness to sacrifice."

The people who matter most in our lives are often the ones who we are willing to sacrifice for. They are the ones who we would do anything for, even if it meant putting our own needs and desires aside. These people may be our family members, close friends, or romantic partners.

While the number of people who really matter to us may be small, the impact they can have on our lives is significant. These are the people who can help us find our purpose in life. They can provide us with the support and encouragement we need to pursue our goals and dreams. They can challenge us to be our best selves and to reach our full potential. They can inspire us to be more compassionate, more empathetic, and more loving.

In order to truly appreciate the people who matter most in our lives, it is important to take the time to cultivate and nurture these relationships. This means being present and attentive when we are with them, actively listening to what they have to say, and showing them that we care through our actions and words. It also means being willing to forgive and to work through challenges and conflicts that may arise.

When we have strong, meaningful connections with the people who matter most in our lives, we are more likely to feel fulfilled and purposeful. These relationships can provide us with a sense of belonging and a feeling that we are making a difference in the world. They can also give us a sense of joy and happiness that is hard to find in other areas of life.

Of course, it is important to remember that relationships are not a one-way street. In order to truly benefit from the people who matter most in our lives, we need to be willing to give as well as receive. This means being there for them when they need us, providing them with support and encouragement, and doing our best to be a positive influence in their lives.

In conclusion, the idea that only a few people are enough to really need is a powerful one. While we may have many acquaintances and casual friendships, it is the people who we have deep, meaningful connections with who truly matter. These are the people who can provide us with a sense of purpose, fulfillment, and joy. By taking the time to cultivate and nurture these relationships, we can truly appreciate the people who matter most in our lives and find a greater sense of purpose in the world.

07

請把你的真誠，
用在真誠的人身上

把我們的真誠投入在真誠的人身上，是尋找人生目標
與意義的重要部分。而所謂真誠，就是一種真心與誠意的
表現，它需要信任與開放才能發展得起來。當我們把真誠
投注於不真誠或不值得的人身上，那我們就是在冒險等著
受傷失望。另一方面，如果我們能夠以誠待人，也就能建
立起有意義的關係，讓我們找到目標、獲得滿足。

那麼，什麼叫做把真誠投入在真誠的人身上？其實就
是要去找出誠實、值得相信、正直可靠的人。因為這些人
會不帶是非判斷地傾聽我們訴說，在需要的時候提供我們

支持與鼓勵，並且與我們同甘共苦。就算再難，這些人也會對我們坦誠以待，而且總是把對我們最有利的事情放在心上。

想把真誠投入在真誠的人身上，需要我們能去覺察自己所建立的關係。這是指在對他人打開心胸之前，願意花時間去了解他們，並且在必要時設定界限。這也表示我們自己必須誠實正直，這樣才能吸引心性相近的人進入我們的生命。

專注於建立深入而有意義的關係，是真誠待人的一個方法。也就是在人際往來上，我們要投入時間與努力，而在跟對方相處時，也要保持參與及關注的態度。這也代表著我們願意分享自己的想法與感受，積極去傾聽他們要說的話。藉由這樣建立深入而有意義的連結，我們就能創造出一種社群意識與歸屬感，進而找到目標、獲得滿足。

待人以誠的另一種方式，則是去尋找與我們的價值觀和目標相同的人。這表示我們要對自己的價值觀與目標很清楚，並能找出跟它們相符的人。同時也要願意去參加與我們價值觀及目標相符合的活動與消遣，這樣才能吸引到志同道合的人進到我們的日常生活之中。

想做到待人以誠，也要能夠去原諒，並且面對我們人際關係中的種種考驗。因為沒有一種關係是完美的，衝突總有發生的時候。然而，如果願意面對這些挑戰，我們就能跟那些真誠而值得相信的人建立起更加穩固而具有意義的關係。

　　總之，待人以誠是找到人生目的和意義很重要的一個部分。這需要我們去找出誠實、值得信賴、正直可靠的人，並與他們建立深刻而有意義的關係。透過把真誠投入在真誠的人身上，我們就能創造出一種社群意識和歸屬感，進而找到目標、獲得滿足。同時，這也代表著為了能跟那些真誠而值得信賴的人建立更加深層的連結，我們將願意去原諒並克服各種關係中的挑戰。

Investing our sincerity in true people is an important part of finding purpose and meaning in life. Sincerity is an expression of our genuine and honest feelings, and it requires trust and openness to truly thrive. When we invest our sincerity in people who are not true or trustworthy, we risk being hurt or let down. On the other hand, when we invest our sincerity in true people, we can build meaningful relationships that can provide us with a sense of purpose and fulfillment.

So, what does it mean to invest our sincerity only in true people? It means seeking out individuals who are honest, trustworthy, and authentic. These are the people who will listen to us without judgment, provide support and encouragement when we need it, and be there for us through thick and thin. They are the people who will be honest with us, even when it's difficult, and who will have our best interests at heart.

Investing our sincerity in true people requires us to be discerning about the relationships we form. It means being willing to take the time to get to know people before opening up to them, and being willing to set boundaries when necessary. It also means being honest and authentic ourselves, so that we can attract like-minded people into our lives.

One way to invest our sincerity in true people is to focus on building deep and meaningful connections. This means investing time and effort into our relationships, and being present and attentive when we are with others. It also means being willing to share our own thoughts and feelings, and to listen actively to what others have to say. By building deep and meaningful connections, we can create a sense of community and belonging that can provide us with a sense of purpose and fulfillment.

Another way to invest our sincerity in true people is to seek out individuals who share our values and goals. This means being clear about our own values and goals, and seeking out people who are aligned with them. It also means being willing to engage in activities and pursuits that are in line with our values and goals, in order to attract like-minded people into our lives.

Investing our sincerity in true people can also involve

being willing to forgive and work through challenges in our relationships. No relationship is perfect, and there will be times when conflicts arise. However, by being willing to work through these challenges, we can build even stronger and more meaningful connections with those who are true and trustworthy.

In conclusion, investing our sincerity in true people is an essential part of finding purpose and meaning in life. It involves seeking out individuals who are honest, trustworthy, and authentic, and building deep and meaningful connections with them. By investing our sincerity in true people, we can create a sense of community and belonging that can provide us with a sense of purpose and fulfillment. It also means being willing to forgive and work through challenges in our relationships, in order to build even stronger connections with those who are true and trustworthy.

08

不要去找別人
來填補自己的缺失

. . . .

在尋找人生目標和意義的過程中，我們可能會很想要找人來把自己所欠缺的補上。因為我們也許深信，如果找到對的夥伴、朋友或良師，就可以從他們身上得到能夠幸福滿足所需要的支持、指引或證明。然而，這個方法很有問題，因為它把能夠幸福滿足的責任推給了其他人，而不在我們自己身上。

那麼，不去追尋能填補我們欠缺的人是什麼意思呢？它代表著我們知道要對自己的幸福與滿足負責，也清楚我們有創造自己想要人生的力量。它也意味著我們能充分掌

握自己的長處與弱點，不斷改進自我，而不是依賴別人來填補缺失。

想要不去找別人來填補所缺，需要我們去開發出對於自我意識與自我信心的覺察。也就是說，要能誠實面對自己的優缺點，也要能針對感到缺乏的地方去改進自我。還要能願意去冒險嘗試新事物，就算超出舒適圈也不怕。

聚焦於建立一種對於自我價值、自我關愛的強大感應力，是避免去找別人來填補自我缺失的一個方法。這代表著要能確知我們生而為人的有形與無形價值，並且願意用善良慈悲來對待自己。這也表示我們願意去建立與他人的界限，並把自己的需要與渴望排在優先。

避免去尋找他人來填補自我缺失的另外一個方法，就是**找出具有支持性而正向的人際關係**。這個意思是指要讓身邊圍繞著能夠鼓舞、啟發我們的人，而不是那些為我們帶來失望的人。這也表示對於自己所在意的人，我們要能坦誠交流，並在有所需要時，願意從他人身上尋求反饋與支持。

終歸來說，**想要避免去找別人來填補所缺，我們就必**

<u>須要對自己的生命負全責，並且願意不斷自我改進。</u>這代表我們清楚自己具有創造所要生活的力量，也知道自己具備達成人生目標與理想的能力。藉由專注於建構優勢，並發展出對於自我價值的強烈感應，我們就能創造出一種在生命中找到目標與滿足感的覺察力，而不會去依賴別人來填補我們的缺失。

In our quest for purpose and meaning in life, it can be tempting to look for someone who can fill in what we lack. We may believe that if we find the right partner, friend, or mentor, they will be able to provide us with the support, guidance, or validation we need to be happy and fulfilled. However, this approach can be problematic, as it places the responsibility for our happiness and fulfillment on someone else, rather than ourselves.

So, what does it mean to not look for someone who can fill in what we lack? It means recognizing that we are responsible for our own happiness and fulfillment, and that we have the power to create the life we want. It means being willing to take ownership of our own strengths and weaknesses, and to work on improving ourselves rather than relying on others to fill in what we lack.

Not looking for someone who can fill in what we lack requires us to develop a sense of self-awareness and self-confidence. It means being honest with ourselves about our strengths and weaknesses, and being willing to work on improving ourselves in areas where we feel lacking. It also means being willing to take risks and try new things, even if they are outside our comfort zone.

One way to avoid looking for someone who can fill in what we lack is to focus on building a strong sense of self-worth and self-love. This means recognizing our own value and worth as individuals, and being willing to treat ourselves with kindness and compassion. It also means being willing to set boundaries with others, and to prioritize our own needs and desires.

Another way to avoid looking for someone who can fill in what we lack is to seek out supportive and positive relationships. This means surrounding ourselves with people who uplift and inspire us, rather than those who bring us down. It also means being willing to communicate openly and honestly with those we care about, and to seek out feedback and support from others when we need it.

Ultimately, not looking for someone who can fill in what we lack is about taking ownership of our own lives and being willing to work on improving ourselves. It means recognizing that we have the power to create the life we want, and that we are capable of achieving our own goals and dreams. By focusing on building our own strengths and developing a strong sense of self-worth, we can create a sense of purpose and fulfillment in our lives, without relying on others to fill in what we lack.

Chpater 2.
找到人生中的滿足感

此圖為AI以書名、目錄和主題為指令而繪製的封面初稿之一。

在這一章，我們將探討幾種技巧，來幫你確定自己想要達成什麼目標，以及要如何進行才能讓一切順利。

首先，重要的是要能理解，你不可能重複「達到目標、再設下一個目標」這樣的動作一直到死。因為人不是機器，想停下來喘口氣、休息、重新充電，是很自然的事。所以你大可往回走一步，重新評估你的優先排序、目標，還有企圖。

接下來，思考一下你究竟想在生命中留下什麼。這就是最重要的目的地。因為你所留下的不僅僅是你生活中的累積，同時也關乎你對他人以及這個世界所造成的影響。它是你所創造的回憶與經驗，你所建立的關係，以及你所帶來的正面改變。

信仰真理的力量，種什麼因，就會得什麼果。當你專

注於自己價值、信念以及原則，也就比較能對自己的狀態覺得滿意，並在生活中感到滿足。

不要習慣性的把跟別人比較、想被人認可的心態拿來找自己麻煩。因為比較心就是「快樂小偷」，我們很容易掉入這個陷阱，並對自己的狀態感到不滿。取而代之的，我們要把焦點放在自己的旅程，並關注究竟已經完成了多少。同時也要去認可我們所達到的成就，不管多麼微小，也要為自己的進展慶賀。

相信專注。當聚焦於自己正在進行的事情，你就會比較能對自己的進展覺得滿意，並且得到一種成就感。這也表示要做到一次只集中精神在一件事情上面，避免分心，並對自己的目標許下承諾。

最後，當你能夠下定決心只去結交一兩個真正的良師益友，那麼也就比較可能擁有一個可以幫助你走在正軌、達到目標的支持網。因為一個好的朋友或人生導師，將能在你最需要的時候供指引、支持以及鼓勵。

藉由專注於自己想要留下什麼、相信真理的力量、避免愛比較、聚焦於專心，並且結交真正的良師益友，你就

能找到一條滿意的路線，達成自己充滿企圖、具有意義的人生目標。

In this chapter, we will explore several techniques that can help you determine what you want to achieve and how to stay satisfied with your progress.

First, it's important to understand that you cannot repeat the task of achieving your goal and setting your next goal until the day you die. Humans are not machines, and it's natural to want to take breaks, rest, and recharge. It's okay to take a step back and reevaluate your priorities, goals, and purpose.

Next, think about what you want to leave behind in your life. This is the most important destination. Your legacy is not just about what you accumulate in life, but about the impact you make on others and the world. It's about the memories and experiences you create, the relationships you build, and the positive change you bring about.

Believe in the power of truth to reap what you sow. When you focus on your values, beliefs, and principles, you are more likely to be satisfied with your progress and feel a sense of fulfillment in your life.

Avoid habitually bothering yourself with comparison and the desire to acknowledge. Comparison is the thief of joy, and it's easy to get caught up in the comparison trap and feel unsatisfied with your progress. Instead, focus on your own journey and what you have accomplished so far. Acknowledge your achievements, no matter how small they may seem, and celebrate your progress.

Believe in concentration. When you concentrate on what you are doing, you are more likely to be satisfied with your progress and feel a sense of accomplishment. This means focusing on one task at a time, avoiding distractions, and committing to your goal.

Finally, when you decide to acquire only one or two true friends or mentors, you are more likely to have a supportive network that will help you stay on track and achieve your goals. A good friend or mentor can offer guidance, support, and encouragement when you need it most.

By focusing on what you want to leave behind, believing in the power of truth, avoiding comparison, focusing on concentration, and acquiring true friends or mentors, you will be able to find a line that you are satisfied with and achieve your goals with purpose and meaning.

09

人生不可能重複「達到目標，再設下一個目標」直到死亡

尋找人生目標是一場不斷進行的旅程；達成目標則是過程中最為意義重大的部分。但我們必須明白，設定目標、達成目標不會是一種機械性的、重複性的工作。因為機器可以不斷去做同樣的動作，但是人不一樣；我們的精力有限，而且我們的動機與優先順序會隨著時間而改變。

我們需要去設定可以達成、具有意義的目標，而且跟我們的價值觀、興趣及抱負相符。這些目標還應該具備彈性、可以改變，允許我們在獲得更多見解與經驗之後，能夠去調整方向及先後順序。

此外，達成目標本身並不是終點。它只是通往更全面、更充實人生的一個步驟。我們也必須認知，**尋找人生目標是一個動態和不斷發展的過程，需要定期自我反思、內省以及修正。**

為了實現人生目標，我們需要在成就與休息之間保持平衡，並且順著這個目標來安排個人福祉與人際關係的優先順序。如果想維持能量與熱情、避免燃燒殆盡，並朝有目標的生活持續邁進，那就得在工作與生活間取得平衡。

有時候，在追求目標和意義的過程中，我們可能會遇到障礙、挑戰或挫折。這些困境可以成為學習、成長和復原的機會。而為了跨越這些障礙並朝有意義的生命旅程邁進，我們大可以去向人生導師、同儕或心理健康專業人員尋求支持。

最後，我們必須了解，人生的意義不在於一個目的地，也不是一個完成品。它是一個自我發現、成長，並對社會做出貢獻的持續進化過程。我們必須擁抱這趟通往自己目標的旅行，去享受過程，並感謝這一路上的各種小小勝利。

總結來說，尋找人生目標是一個不斷發展和演變的過程，需要去設定並實現有意義的目標，保持工作和個人生活之間的平衡，適應變化，尋求支持，並擁抱這趟旅程。我們也必須清楚自己不是機器，這樣才能並按照人生目標來排出個人福祉與人際關係的優先順序。

The pursuit of finding one's purpose in life is an ongoing journey, and achieving a goal is a significant part of that process. However, it's essential to understand that setting and achieving goals can't be a mechanical, repetitive task. While machines may perform the same task repeatedly, human beings are different; we have a limited amount of energy, and our motivation and priorities change over time.

People need to set achievable and meaningful goals that align with their values, interests, and aspirations. Goals should also be flexible and adaptable, allowing individuals to adjust their direction and priorities as they gain more insights and experiences.

Moreover, achieving a goal is not an endpoint in itself. It's a step towards a more comprehensive and fulfilling purpose in life. People must recognize that finding purpose in life is a dynamic and evolving process, and it requires regular self-reflection, introspection, and course correction.

To achieve the purpose of life, individuals must maintain a balance between achievement and rest, and they must prioritize their well-being and relationships along with their goals. A healthy balance between work and personal life is essential to maintain energy and motivation, avoid burnout, and sustain progress towards purposeful living.

At times, individuals may encounter obstacles, challenges, or setbacks in their pursuit of goals and purpose. These challenges can be opportunities for learning, growth, and resilience. People can seek support from mentors, peers, or mental health professionals to overcome these hurdles and continue their journey towards purposeful living.

Finally, individuals must understand that the purpose of life is not a destination or a final product. It's an ongoing process of self-discovery, growth, and contribution to society. Individuals must embrace the journey towards their purpose, enjoy the process, and appreciate the small victories along the way.

In summary, finding the purpose of life is a dynamic and evolving process that requires setting and achieving meaningful goals, maintaining a balance between work and personal life, adapting to changes, seeking support, and embracing the journey. People must recognize that they are not machines and prioritize their well-being and relationships along with their goals.

10

捨棄不必要的事物，
才能看見生命中真正寶貴的目標

··

　　找到人生目標是一個複雜的過程，通常涉及更多的面向，而不僅僅是設定目標並努力實現而已。像有些時候，為了找到目標，我們就必須放棄不再對我們有益的特定事物。從消極的想法、負面的信仰，到不健康的人際關係、不得志的工作，這種種一切都有可能。

　　想辨別出我們想拋棄什麼，需要自我省思並對自己誠實。我們必須自問，什麼是我們真正重視的，什麼能帶給我們快樂與滿足，什麼又會對我們造成壓力與焦慮。我們可能需要去檢視自己的人際關係、嗜好興趣，以及日常中

的例行公事，以便確認我們需要放棄什麼才能向前邁進。

一旦找出要拋下的事物，我們就要刻意去進行。這會是一個充滿挑戰的過程，也可能需要我們去面對不舒服的真相，無論關於自己或是他人。但這就是朝向找到目標極為必要的一步。

我們必須記住，放手從來都不是件容易的事。這需要時間和努力，而且一路上也可能多所挫折。但這是趟值得的旅程，因為它讓我們成長，並邁向更充實的人生。

在某些情況下，放手可能代表著要做出困難的選擇，例如結束一段有害的關係，或離開不再帶為我們帶來喜悅的工作。但重要的是，**我們必須以自己的幸福和快樂為優先，而不是別人的期望或義務。**

當我們放下不再對我們有益的事物，就能為新的經驗、關係和機會創造空間，讓它們進入我們的生命之中。我們可以專注於對自己真正重要的事情，並讓目標、行動能與我們的價值觀和熱情相符。

總而言之，想要找到人生目標，就要放下對我們不再

有益的事物。包括負面的想法和信仰、不健康的關係、不得志的工作。這需要自我反省、誠實,並且做出向前邁進的打算。雖然這可能極具挑戰性,但放手能為新的經驗、關係和機會創造空間、讓它們進入我們的生活,進而幫助我們找到更加充實、更具意義的存在。

Discovering one's purpose in life is a complex process that often involves more than just setting goals and striving towards them. Sometimes, to find our purpose, we must also let go of certain things that no longer serve us. This could be anything from negative thoughts and beliefs to unhealthy relationships or unfulfilling jobs.

Identifying what we want to leave behind requires self-reflection and honesty. We must ask ourselves what we truly value, what brings us joy and fulfillment, and what causes us stress and anxiety. We may need to examine our relationships, habits, and daily routines to determine what we need to let go of to move forward.

Once we have identified what we want to leave behind, we need to set the intention to do so. This can be a challenging process, and it may require us to face uncomfortable truths about ourselves or others. But it is a necessary step towards finding our purpose.

It's important to remember that letting go of things is not always easy. It may take time and effort, and there may be setbacks along the way. But it is a journey that is worth taking, as it allows us to grow and move towards a more fulfilling life.

In some cases, letting go may mean making difficult choices, such as ending a toxic relationship or leaving a job that no longer brings us joy. But it's essential to prioritize our own well-being and happiness over external expectations or obligations.

As we let go of what no longer serves us, we create space for new experiences, relationships, and opportunities to come into our lives. We can focus on what truly matters to us and align our goals and actions with our values and passions.

In conclusion, finding our purpose in life often involves letting go of what no longer serves us. This could be negative thoughts and beliefs, unhealthy relationships, or unfulfilling jobs. It requires self-reflection, honesty, and setting intentions to move forward. Although it may be challenging, letting go creates space for new experiences, relationships, and opportunities to come into our lives, helping us find a more fulfilling and purposeful existence.

要相信「種什麼因、
得什麼果」是真理

對於「種什麼因、得什麼果」這個真理的信仰,是許多精神與哲學傳統的基本原則。它暗示著我們所做出的選擇以及所採取的行動,將會對我們的未來造成結果。換句話說,我們的思想、言語及行為,塑造出我們的命運。

這個原則提醒我們,我們不是境遇的受害者,而是現實的創造者。我們有權力去選擇我們的想法和行動,而這些選擇則形成了我們生命的軌跡。如果我們播下正向行動與思考的種子,就比較可能得到正向的收穫;至於負面的行動和思考,就可能會帶來負面的後果。

這個原則的力量體現於一個事實，就是它促進個人的責任與擔當。**我們必須掌握自己的選擇及結果，而不是為了我們的問題而去指責他人或外部環境。**藉由這樣做，我們就能獲得一種對自己生活的主導性與控制感，進而感到自主而解放。

相信「種什麼因、得什麼果」的力量也需要培養自我意識及正念。我們要能對自己的想法、情感和行為有所覺察，並知道它們如何影響自己與他人。這種意識可以幫助我們做出更好的選擇，並且更有決心、有目標的去行動。

此外，這個原則也提醒我們萬物相互關聯。**我們的行為和選擇不是存在於真空之中，而是具有漣漪效應，會對我們身邊其他人及整個世界產生影響。**因此，我們必須用一種不只對我們自己有利、也能對身邊的人有益的方式，來思考我們做出選擇與採取行動之後的廣泛牽連。

總之，相信「種什麼因、得什麼果」的力量是強大的信念，提醒我們對形塑自己生活的自主性與責任感。它需要我們去培養自覺，能有決心、有目標的去行動，並且意識到萬物相互聯繫。透過這樣，我們可以創造出更充實、更有意義的生活，並為創建更加正面的世界有所貢獻。

The belief in the power of truth that "I reap what I sow" is a fundamental principle in many spiritual and philosophical traditions. It suggests that the choices we make and the actions we take have consequences that determine our future. In other words, our thoughts, words, and deeds shape our destiny.

This principle reminds us that we are not victims of circumstance, but rather creators of our own reality. We have the power to choose our thoughts and actions, and these choices shape the trajectory of our lives. If we sow positive actions and thoughts, we are more likely to reap positive outcomes, while negative actions and thoughts may lead to negative consequences.

The power of this principle lies in the fact that it promotes personal responsibility and accountability. Instead of blaming others or external circumstances for our problems, we must take ownership of our choices and their consequences. By doing so, we gain a sense of agency and control over our lives, which can be empowering and liberating.

Believing in the power of "I reap what I sow" also requires us to cultivate self-awareness and mindfulness. We must be aware of our thoughts, feelings, and behaviors, and how they impact ourselves and others. This awareness can help us make better choices and act with more intention and purpose.

Furthermore, this principle reminds us of the interconnectedness of all things. Our actions and choices do not exist in a vacuum, but rather have ripple effects that can impact others and the world around us. Therefore, we must consider the wider implications of our choices and act in ways that benefit not only ourselves but also those around us.

In conclusion, the belief in the power of truth that "I reap what I sow" is a powerful principle that reminds us of our agency and responsibility in shaping our lives. It requires us to cultivate self-awareness and act with intention and purpose, recognizing the interconnectedness of all things. By doing so, we can create a more fulfilling and purposeful existence, and contribute to a more positive world.

12

避免掉入「比較」
與「認同」的陷阱

· ·

在現代社會中，人們很容易陷入與他人比較以及尋求外在認同的陷阱。然而，這將成為我們尋找人生目標、實現滿足感的一大障礙。因為它會導致自卑、嫉妒，還有一種我們跟別人格格不入的孤立感。

為了避開這個陷阱，我們必須培養一種接受自己、善待自己的心態。要知道，每個人都是獨特的個體，擁有自己的優點、缺點，以及自己的人生道路。拿自己去跟他人比較，不僅對自己不公平，而且根本白做工，因為我們永遠無法真正了解別人的掙扎、挑戰，以及經歷過什麼。

而且，追求他人的認可和贊同，還會導致滑坡效應，讓人掉入一個永無止境尋找「驗證」的循環。當我們受到讚揚或認同，可能會感到暫時的滿足，但這樣的感受往往相當短促，很快地我們就又會發現自己不斷追求更多。

要擺脫這種循環，我們必須學會從「我們是誰」去珍視自己的價值，不受外界眼光的影響。我們要能從自己的成就與進步中尋找喜悅與滿足，而不是苦求他人的認可。

這需要一種心態的轉變，也正是我們要學會聚焦於自己的成長，而不要去跟別人做比較。同時還必須學會欣賞他人的特質與長處，並且不會因此而感到受威脅，或是覺得自己不夠好。

此外，建立人生目標意識也要跟我們的價值觀、熱情所在以及具體目標一致，而不是一直拿自己去跟其他人相比。藉由聚焦於真正重要的事物，我們就能在生活中開創方向感與意義。

總之，很重要的是不要養成跟別人比較、追求外部認同的習慣。想要找到人生目標、獲得滿足，就要培養接受、善待自己的心態，並把精力放在自身的成長與進步

上。藉由讓價值觀、熱情與目標達到一致，我們就能創造出一種在生活中找到方向與意義的意識，而不去依賴外在的證明。

In our modern world, it's easy to fall into the trap of comparing ourselves to others and seeking recognition or approval from external sources. However, this can be a major obstacle in our search for purpose and fulfillment. It can lead to feelings of inadequacy, jealousy, and a sense of disconnection from ourselves and others.

To avoid this trap, we must cultivate a mindset of self-acceptance and self-compassion. We must recognize that we are unique individuals with our own strengths, weaknesses, and path in life. Comparing ourselves to others is not only unfair to ourselves, but it's also an exercise in futility, as we can never truly know the struggles, challenges, and experiences of others.

Furthermore, seeking recognition or approval from others can be a slippery slope that leads to a never-ending cycle of validation seeking. We may feel temporary satisfaction when we receive praise or recognition, but it's often short-lived, and we may find ourselves continually seeking more.

To break free from this cycle, we must learn to value

ourselves for who we are, regardless of external validation. We must find joy and fulfillment in our own accomplishments and progress, rather than seeking validation from others.

This requires a shift in mindset, where we learn to focus on our own growth, rather than comparing ourselves to others. We must also learn to appreciate the unique qualities and strengths of others, without feeling threatened or inadequate.

Moreover, cultivating a sense of purpose in life involves aligning our values, passions, and goals, rather than comparing ourselves to others. By focusing on what truly matters to us, we can create a sense of direction and meaning in our lives.

In conclusion, it's important to avoid the habit of comparing ourselves to others and seeking recognition or approval from external sources. To find purpose and fulfillment in life, we must cultivate a mindset of self-acceptance, self-compassion, and focus on our own growth and progress. By aligning our values, passions, and goals, we can create a sense of direction and meaning in our lives that is not dependent on external validation.

13

請 相 信 專 注 的 力 量

　　相信專注力是尋找人生目標、獲得實現滿足的重要元件。「專注」是指能夠把注意力聚焦在特定任務或事物上、而不被外在或內在刺激分心的一種能力。這是項基本技能，讓我們得以實現目標，對於個人成就及事業成功來說都很重要。

　　專注的力量在於一種能力，它幫助我們達到一種化境狀態，就是完全沉浸於手上的任務之中，並且對於時間的感知以及自我的意識都大為降低。若想達到成就巔峰，這個狀態至為重要，因為它讓我們能夠發揮所有潛力。

專注也讓我們能對某項事務或技能去發展出較為深層的理解與掌握。藉由把注意力集中，我們可以更有效率的吸收訊息，去辨識出模式與連結，並且發展出嶄新的見解與構想。

對於專注力的信仰，需要我們培養出一種正念而用心的方式去面對日常生活。**我們必須對來自於內在與外在的分心有所意識，並且學會有效率地管理它們。**而這可能會跟冥想、正念以及其他形式的心理訓練有關。

此外，我們也必須學會優先考慮自己的目標，並消除那些無助於目標的干擾。這可能意味著要拒絕某些活動，對他人設定界限，並且減少使用科技或社群媒體。

專注力還需要我們去培養一種成長的心態，讓我們能把挑戰和障礙視為學習與成長的機會。當我們遇到困難，不會灰心或放棄，而會運用我們的專心與注意力來克服它們，進而發展出韌性。

總之，相信專注的力量是尋找人生目標並獲得實現滿足的基本要件。**透過開發集中注意力及管理干擾的能力，我們可以達到一種全神貫注的化境，加深我們對於技能和**

事物的理解與掌握，並且能以韌性去克服障礙。而培養一種正念而用心的方式去生活，並優先考慮我們的目標，就是發展專注力並讓我們所有潛能得以解鎖的重要關鍵。

Believing in the power of concentration is a crucial component of finding purpose and fulfillment in life. Concentration is the ability to focus one's attention on a specific task or object, without being distracted by external or internal stimuli. It is a fundamental skill that allows us to achieve our goals, and it is essential for personal and professional success.

The power of concentration lies in its ability to help us achieve a state of flow, where we are fully immersed in the task at hand, and our sense of time and self-awareness is diminished. This state of flow is essential for achieving peak performance, and it allows us to tap into our full potential.

Concentration also enables us to develop deeper levels of understanding and mastery of a subject or skill. By focusing our attention, we can absorb information more effectively, identify patterns and connections, and develop new insights and ideas.

Believing in the power of concentration requires us to cultivate a mindful and intentional approach to our daily lives. We must be aware of our internal and external distractions and learn to manage them effectively. This may involve techniques such as meditation, mindfulness, or other forms of mental training.

Moreover, we must learn to prioritize our goals and eliminate distractions that do not serve our purpose. This may mean saying no to certain activities, setting boundaries with others, or reducing our exposure to technology and social media.

The power of concentration also requires us to cultivate a growth mindset, where we view challenges and obstacles as opportunities for learning and growth. Rather than becoming discouraged or giving up when we encounter difficulties, we must use our concentration and focus to overcome them and develop resilience.

In conclusion, believing in the power of concentration is a fundamental component of finding purpose and fulfillment in life. By developing the ability to focus our attention and manage distractions, we can achieve a state of flow, deepen our understanding and mastery of skills and subjects, and overcome obstacles with resilience. Cultivating a mindful and intentional approach to our daily lives and prioritizing our goals is essential for developing the power of concentration and unlocking our full potential.

14

我們只需要一兩位
真正的朋友與人生導師

與他人建立良好關係是尋找人生目的與得到滿足的基本要素。然而,重要的是要知道,並非所有關係都對我們的生活具有同等影響力。事實上,擁有太多關係可能會讓我們不知所措,並且也未必能夠提供我們真正所需連結的深度與品質。

因此,決定只尋求一兩位真正的朋友或人生導師,能為我們提供所需支持、指引與理解,是很重要的。這些人應該是我們信任、尊重和欽佩的人,並且與我們分享相同的價值觀、熱情與目標。

擁有一小群親密的朋友或人生導師，可以為我們提供一種社群意識和歸屬感，同時也是我們靈感和動力的來源。他們可以幫助我們應對生活的挑戰，提供反饋和建議，並一起慶祝我們的成功和里程碑。

　　然而，選擇這些人不能輕率行事。我們必須用心思考並仔細抉擇，去選出與我們的價值觀和目標相符的人。這可能需要花時間去認識人，建立關係，並評估這些連結的品質。

　　此外，我們必須清楚，在人際關係上質比量更重要。因為光是認識一堆人或只是表面上的聯繫，可能無法提供我們真正所需連結的深度及支持。也因此，重要的是要把時間和精力投注在去跟少數精選過的人建立有意義而真誠的關係上。

　　最後，只有一兩個親近的朋友或人生導師，並不表示我們應該孤立自己。保持對他人的開放性與好奇心很重要，而在需要時，我們也要願意去耕耘新關係和連結。但無論如何，擁有一個小群良師益友，能夠給予我們所需的基礎與支持，讓我們得以在種種生活挑戰之中航行，並且找到人生的目標。

總之，**決定只跟少數真正的朋友或人生導師交往，能為我們尋找目標、獲得滿足帶來所需關係的深度與品質。**這需要用心而慎重地選擇，並且也要願意投入時間和精力去建立有意義的關係。因為擁有一小群良師益友，就能為我們提供社群意識、支持與靈感，幫助我們以韌性和決心去應對生活中的種種挑戰。

Having strong relationships with others is a fundamental component of finding purpose and fulfillment in life. However, it's important to recognize that not all relationships are equal in terms of their impact on our lives. In fact, having too many relationships can be overwhelming and may not provide the depth and quality of connection that we truly need.

Therefore, it's essential to decide to get only one or two true friends or mentors who can provide us with the support, guidance, and understanding that we need. These individuals should be people we trust, respect, and admire, and who share our values, passions, and goals.

Having a small group of close friends or mentors can provide us with a sense of community and belonging, as well as a source of inspiration and motivation. They can help us navigate life's challenges, provide feedback and advice, and celebrate our successes and milestones.

However, choosing these individuals should not be taken lightly. We must be intentional and thoughtful in our selection, and choose individuals who are aligned with our values and goals. This may involve taking the time to get to know people, building rapport, and evaluating the quality of the connection.

Moreover, we must recognize that the quality of our relationships is more important than the quantity. Having many acquaintances or superficial connections may not provide the depth of connection and support that we truly need. Therefore, it's essential to invest time and energy in building meaningful and authentic relationships with a few select individuals.

Finally, having one or two close friends or mentors does not mean that we should isolate ourselves from others. It's important to maintain a sense of openness and curiosity towards others, and to be willing to cultivate new relationships and connections as needed. However, having a small group of close friends or mentors can provide us with the foundation and support that we need to navigate life's challenges and find our purpose in life.

In conclusion, deciding to get only one or two true friends or mentors can provide us with the depth and quality of connection that we need to find purpose and fulfillment in life. It requires intentional and thoughtful selection, as well as a willingness to invest time and energy in building meaningful relationships. Having a small group of close friends or mentors can provide us with a sense of community, support, and inspiration, and can help us navigate life's challenges with resilience and determination.

15

不知道就是「不知道」，
知道就是「知道」

了解自己所知與所不知的能力，是尋找目標、獲得滿
足的重要元素。這需要具備一定程度的自我意識、謙遜的
態度，以及一種對於學習與成長的意願。

當我們不知道答案時就說「我不知道」，是一種展現
誠實與脆弱的有力形式。它說明了我們並非萬無缺失，並
且總是有成長與進步的空間。也在我們尋找新資訊與觀點
時，提供一個學習與發現的機會。

另一方面，承認我們知道什麼也很重要。因為它讓我

們認識到自己的優勢、技能與專長、得以運用這些來實現我們的目標，並且對周遭的世界做出貢獻。

認識自己知與不知的能力，需要我們培養成長心態，把挑戰和障礙視為學習與進步的機會。我們必須願意提出問題、尋找新知及觀點，並且在不知道答案時勇於承認。

此外，還有一點很重要，就是認識到可能有些事情我們並不知道自己不知道。換句話說，也就是在我們的知識與理解中，可能存在著盲點或缺陷，但連我們自己都沒有意識到。而想要對這一點有所認知，就需要一定程度的謙虛與開放性，來面對反饋意見與新的體驗。

為了克服這些盲點，我們必須願意尋求多元的觀點和意見，挑戰自己的假設和信念，並且願意接受反饋意見以及建設性的批評。而這可能會需要尋找人生導師、與不同背景和見解的人交往，並讓自己多接觸新的體驗和挑戰。

清楚理解到我們所知道與不知道的事情，是尋找及實現人生目標的重要元件。這需要謙遜、誠實，以及一種去面對學習和成長的願意。透過承認自己不知道的事，我們可以尋求新的訊息與觀點，並且發展新的技能和專長。而

藉由確知自己所知道的事，我們則可以利用優勢和技能來實現目標，並為周遭的世界做出貢獻。最後，若能意識到可能有些事情我們並不知道自己不知道，那麼就能培養成長思維方式，並且以開放的態度去面對新的經驗和觀點。

The ability to recognize what we know and what we don't know is an essential component of finding purpose and fulfillment in life. It requires a level of self-awareness and humility, as well as a willingness to learn and grow.

Saying "I don't know" when we don't have the answer is a powerful form of honesty and vulnerability. It acknowledges that we are not infallible, and that there is always room for growth and development. It also provides an opportunity for learning and discovery, as we seek out new information and perspectives.

On the other hand, acknowledging what we do know is also important. It allows us to recognize our strengths, skills, and expertise, and to leverage these to achieve our goals and contribute to the world around us.

The ability to recognize what we know and what we don't know requires us to cultivate a growth mindset, where we view challenges and obstacles as opportunities for learning and development. We must be willing to ask questions, seek out new information and perspectives, and admit when we don't have the answer.

Moreover, it's important to recognize that there may be things we don't know that we don't know. In other words, there may be blind spots or gaps in our knowledge and understanding that we are not even aware of. Recognizing this requires a level of humility and openness to feedback and new experiences.

In order to overcome these blind spots, we must be willing to seek out diverse perspectives and opinions, challenge our own assumptions and beliefs, and be open to feedback and constructive criticism. This may involve seeking out mentors, engaging with people from different backgrounds and perspectives, and exposing ourselves to new experiences and challenges.

Having insight into what we know and what we don't know is a crucial component of finding purpose and fulfillment in life. It requires humility, honesty, and a willingness to learn and grow. By acknowledging what we don't know, we can seek out new information and perspectives, and develop new skills and expertise. By recognizing what we do know, we can leverage our strengths and skills to achieve our goals and contribute to the world around us. Finally, by acknowledging that there may be things we don't know that we don't know, we can cultivate a growth mindset and be open to new experiences and perspectives.

16

學會學習的方法，
才能找到更深層次的目標

「學習」是找到人生目標、獲得實現滿足的重要成分。它讓我們發展新的技能、知識和觀點，並擴展我們對周遭世界的理解。然而，為了真正發揮學習的力量，我們首先必須「學習如何學習」。

「學習如何學習」包括發展一整套技巧和策略，讓我們能有效獲取並記憶新的資訊。這些技巧包括批判性思維、解決問題、創造力及溝通，還有做筆記、保持記憶力與時間管理的方法。

除了發展這些技法之外，我們還必須培養一種成長的心態，去把挑戰和障礙視為學習和進步的機會。這需要我們能對新的體驗和觀點抱持開放性，並以好奇心和熱情來面對學習。

此外，很重要的是要知道，學習並不是一種適用於所有人的方法。因為**不同的人有不同的學習風格，所以對一個人有效的方法可能對另一個人無效**。也因此，我們必須願意去嘗試不同的技巧和策略，並在需要時去做出適當的調整。

一些有效的學習策略包括將複雜的資訊分解得更小、更易於處理，使用記憶法或其他記憶技巧來幫助記住資訊，並且尋求多樣化的觀點和意見來加深我們的理解。

同時，我們也必須意識到**學習不是一次性的事件，而是一個不斷發展的過程**。為了真正掌握學習的力量，我們必須致力於終身學習和個人發展。這需要一種好奇心、嘗試新鮮事物的意願，以及對於持續成長與進步的承諾。

總之，學習是尋找目標、實現滿足的基本元素。學習如何學習涉及開發一套技巧與策略，讓我們能有效獲取並

保留新訊息，同時也要去培養成長思維，以及對於終身學習的承諾。藉由抱持好奇心與熱情來對待學習，並願意去嘗試不同的技巧和策略，我們就能擴展對周遭世界的理解，發展新的技能和知識，並在生活中找到更深層次的目標和意義。

Learning is an essential component of finding purpose and fulfillment in life. It allows us to develop new skills, knowledge, and perspectives, and to expand our understanding of the world around us. However, in order to truly harness the power of learning, we must first learn how to learn.

Learning how to learn involves developing a set of skills and strategies that enable us to acquire and retain new information effectively. These skills include critical thinking, problem-solving, creativity, and communication, as well as techniques for note-taking, memory retention, and time management.

In addition to developing these skills, we must also cultivate a growth mindset, where we view challenges and obstacles as opportunities for learning and development. This requires us to be open to new experiences and perspectives, and to approach learning with curiosity and enthusiasm.

Moreover, it's important to recognize that learning is not a one-size-fits-all approach. Different people have different learning styles, and what works for one person may not work for another. Therefore, we must be willing to experiment with different techniques and strategies, and be willing to adapt and adjust as needed.

Some effective strategies for learning include breaking down complex information into smaller, more manageable chunks, using mnemonics and other memory techniques to help retain information, and seeking out diverse perspectives and opinions to deepen our understanding.

It's also important to recognize that learning is not a one-time event, but rather a continuous process. In order to truly harness the power of learning, we must be committed to lifelong learning and personal development. This requires a sense of curiosity, a willingness to try new things, and a commitment to ongoing growth and development.

In conclusion, learning is a fundamental component of finding purpose and fulfillment in life. Learning how to learn involves developing a set of skills and strategies that enable us to acquire and retain new information effectively, as well as cultivating a growth mindset and commitment to lifelong learning. By approaching learning with curiosity and enthusiasm, and being willing to experiment with different techniques and strategies, we can expand our understanding of the world around us, develop new skills and knowledge, and find deeper purpose and meaning in our live.

Chpater 3.
讓自己開心度過每一天

此圖為AI以書名、目錄和主題為指令而繪製的封面初稿之一。

第三章要把重點放在一個概念上，就是用快樂來填滿每一天。眾所皆知，幸福感是充實生命的關鍵元素，至於我們花時間的方式，則對整體幸福感扮演著非常重要的角色。在這個章節中，我們將探討幾個主題，來幫助自己在日常生活中獲得更大的幸福感。

　　第一個要討論的主題是「昨天對個人影響最大」的想法。這個概念很重要，因為我們過往的經歷塑造出今天的我們之所以是誰，並會對我們的全面幸福造成影響。如果過去曾經有過負面經驗，那我們就可能會難以維持對生活的正向展望。然而，要緊的是聚焦於當下與未來，並且努力放下那些可能會阻止我們發展的負面經驗。

　　下一個要談的主題是「早晨的習慣決定一整天的命運」。這是一個重要觀念，因為如何開啟一天將會為我們接下來的一整天定調。而充滿正能量的晨間例行活動，例

如做運動、靜坐冥想或是寫日誌，不僅有助減輕壓力和焦慮，也能為快樂而充滿生產力的一天做好準備。

另一個要討論的重要議題則是「專注於自己的幸福，把它放在第一位，只要不傷害到其他人」。這個觀念很關鍵，因為許多人會把別人的需求放在自己之上，以至於產生疲憊、很不快樂的感覺。而透過將自己的幸福放在優先位置，我們不但可以把自己照顧得比較好，也能因此而更加關注他人。

缺乏某些東西而造成某種行為模式、傾向、特殊追求或行動目的，則是另一個要討論的概念。因為這個概念認為，當我們在生活中有所欠缺時，我們可能會發展出某種行為模式或傾向去追求那些事物、產生一種目標意識。而對於那些期望在生命中找到目標與幸福的人來說，這可能會是一個強大的動力。

另一個要探討的重要議題是「最幸福的時刻就是現在」。這是一個基本原則，因為許多人活在過去或未來，而這會導致後悔、焦慮或不確定的感覺。透過關注當下並在簡單的生活事物中找到喜悅，我們就能活得更加充實、更為快樂。你得帶著一個想法，就是幾乎對於所有情況，

你都可以有一大堆的想像。而藉由去想像什麼是我們要的並且設定目標，我們就能努力朝向去創造一種能為我們帶來喜悅與滿足感的充實生活。

針對如何在生活中填滿快樂，第三章提供了寶貴的見解與實用的提示。透過聚焦於這一章所概述的主題，我們將可以努力在日常生活中找到更大的目標與幸福。

Chapter 3 focuses on the idea of filling one's day with happiness. It is no secret that happiness is a crucial element of a fulfilling life, and the way we spend our time plays a critical role in our overall happiness. In this chapter, you explore several topics that will help readers achieve greater happiness in their daily lives.

The first topic you explore is the idea that yesterday has the greatest impact on the individual. This is an important concept because our past experiences shape who we are today, and they can affect our overall level of happiness. If we have had negative experiences in the past, it can be challenging to maintain a positive outlook on life. However, it is essential to focus on the present and future and work to let go of negative experiences that may be holding us back.

The next topic you address is the idea that a morning routine determines the whole day. This is an important concept because how we start our day can set the tone for the rest of the day. A positive morning routine that includes exercise, meditation, or journaling can help to reduce stress and anxiety and set the stage for a happy and productive day.

Another essential topic you cover is the importance of focusing on one's happiness and putting it first, as long as it does not harm others. This is a critical concept because many people prioritize the needs of others over their own, leading to feelings of burnout and unhappiness. By prioritizing our own happiness, we can take better care of ourselves and, in turn, be more present for others.

The idea that a lack of something makes a pattern, inclination, pursuit, and purpose of action is another essential topic you address. This concept suggests that when we lack something in our lives, we may develop a pattern of behavior or inclination towards pursuing that thing, leading to a sense of purpose. This can be a powerful motivator for people looking to find purpose and happiness in their lives.

Another key topic you explore is the idea that the happiest time is now. This is an essential concept because many people live in the past or future, which can lead to feelings of regret, anxiety, or uncertainty. By focusing on the present moment and finding joy in the simple things in life, we can live more fully and happily. You address the idea that there is probably a lump of your imagination in almost every case. By imagining what we want and setting goals, we can work towards creating a fulfilling life that brings us joy and satisfaction.

Chapter 3 offers valuable insights and practical tips for filling one's day with happiness. By focusing on the topics outlined in this chapter, readers can work towards finding greater purpose and joy in their daily lives.

17

昨 天 對 個 人 的 影 響 最 大

在尋找人生目標的過程中，很重要的是去觀照我們的過往經歷，以便了解它們究竟如何塑造出我們的現在與未來。而「昨天對個人影響最大」的想法，則點出了一個概念，就是我們的過去對於我們今天之所以是什麼樣的人，具有深遠的影響。

我們的過往經歷可能是正面的，也可能是負面的。正面經驗能帶給我們未來充滿信心與希望的感覺。而負面的經驗則可能會導致恐懼、焦慮以及不確定感的產生。在許多情況下，比起正面經驗，負面經驗可能會對我們的生活帶來更巨大的衝擊，因為它們會留下持續性的傷痕，需要

時間去平復。

我們必須有所認知，過往的經驗沒有辦法全然在我們的掌控之中。我們也許曾經歷創傷、霸凌或其他負面事件，以至於留下很深的感情傷口。這些傷可能會影響我們的人際關係、自尊心，以及對於人生目標的整體意識。

學習如何放下負面情緒以及對我們無益的行為模式，是面對過往經歷的挑戰之一。對某些人來說，這可能需要尋求治療或其他形式的專業幫助，才能逐步解決過去的創傷，並發展出健康的應對機制。

很重要的是要知道，**過去的經歷並不一定真的能夠定義我們。**因為我們有能力去創造自己的命運，讓生活變成想要的樣子。而藉由專注當下和未來，並朝著目標努力，我們就能開始克服過往經驗的負面影響，進而創造更有意義的生活。

克服負面經驗帶來影響的一個方法，就是重新去建構我們對於這些經驗的想法。**比起把自己視為過去的犧牲者，我們大可選擇把這些經驗當作是成長與學習的機會。**藉由擁抱一種成長的心態，我們就能發展出復原力，並且

在逆境中學習茁壯。

另一個克服負面經歷的必要面向，則是去開發一種善待自己的意識。很基本的是要知道，我們並不完美，犯錯沒有關係。藉由對自己寬容慈悲，我們就能在自我尊重與自我成長上有更好的發展。

總之，「昨天對個人影響最大」說明了一點，就是我們何以變成今天的模樣，過往經歷扮演著很重要的角色。儘管負面經驗可能很難克服，但它們並無法真正定義我們。藉由關注當下與未來，重新建構我們的想法，並且善待自己，我們就能征服過往經歷帶來的負面效應，並且創造更加充實的生活。

In the quest for finding purpose in life, it's essential to look at our past experiences to understand how they shape our present and future. The idea that yesterday has the greatest impact on individuals speaks to the notion that our past experiences have a profound influence on who we are today.

Our past experiences can be both positive and negative. Positive experiences can give us a sense of confidence and hope for the future, while negative experiences can create fear, anxiety, and uncertainty. In many cases, negative experiences can have a more significant impact on our lives than positive ones, as they can leave lasting scars that take time to heal.

It's important to recognize that our past experiences are not always entirely within our control. We may have experienced trauma, abuse, or other negative events that have left us with deep emotional wounds. These wounds can affect our relationships, our self-esteem, and our overall sense of purpose in life.

One of the challenges of dealing with the impact of our past experiences is learning how to let go of negative emotions and patterns of behavior that no longer serve us. For some, this may involve seeking therapy or other forms of professional help to work through past trauma and develop healthy coping mechanisms.

It's important to recognize that our past experiences do not have to define us. We have the power to create our own destiny and make our lives into whatever we want them to be. By focusing on the present and future and working towards our goals, we can begin to overcome the negative effects of our past experiences and create a more fulfilling life.

One way to overcome the impact of negative past experiences is to reframe our thinking around them. Rather than seeing ourselves as victims of our past, we can choose to view our experiences as opportunities for growth and learning. By embracing a growth mindset, we can develop resilience and learn to thrive in the face of adversity.

Another essential aspect of overcoming the impact

of negative past experiences is developing a sense of self-compassion. It's essential to recognize that we are not perfect and that it's okay to make mistakes. By being kind and compassionate to ourselves, we can develop greater self-esteem and self-worth.

In conclusion, the idea that yesterday has the greatest impact on individuals speaks to the notion that our past experiences play a critical role in shaping who we are today. While negative past experiences can be challenging to overcome, they do not have to define us. By focusing on the present and future, reframing our thinking, and developing self-compassion, we can overcome the negative effects of our past experiences and create a more fulfilling life.

18

早晨的習慣
決定一整天的命運

我們開始一天的方式，會為接下來的整天定下基調；而我們的晨間習慣，則在整體幸福感與目標的確立上，扮演了關鍵性的角色。早上的例行活動能為整天定調的概念，說明了養成良好習慣與的日行工作的重要性，因為這對我們的身體、心理、以及精神層面都有所助益。

許多成功人士相信，晨間習慣有益於他們對於自己的產能與成就做好準備。舉例來說，很多企業家與商務領導人會固定早起，把一天開始的最初幾個小時用在運動、冥想，或是其他形式的自我照管上。藉由把自己的福祉與關

照放在優先，他們一整天下來就比較能夠專注於自己的工作，並且達成目標。

培養良好的早晨習慣不僅有益於實現專業成功，也對支持全面性的心理與身體健康有好處。 許多專家都建議用運動來開始一天，因為它能幫助提升情緒、能量層次以及整體幸福感。其他常見的晨間例行活動則包括寫日誌、冥想、閱讀，或是投入於一些具有創造性、能帶來快樂與滿足感的嗜好之中。

基於個人的需要與偏好不同，良好晨間習慣的具體元素也有所差異。然而，確實有幾項共同元素，往往容易帶來較為成功而充實的晨間時光。而這些元素則包括：每天都在固定時間起床、避免一早就使用電子設備、喝水或茶、從事身體性的活動、為這天訂下計畫，還有抱持正念與感謝。

培養良好晨間習慣的挑戰之一，就是找出時間和動力去做。因為對某些人來說，這可能需要比平常早起或改變其它生活方式，才能做到把自我關照放在優先。然而，良好晨間習慣所能帶來的好處，其實非常值得這些努力，因為它們能提升生產力、創造力，以及全面性的福祉。

總之，「晨間習慣決定一整天走向」說明了一件事的重要性，就是要去建立能對我們身心靈有所幫助的良好習慣與例行活動。藉由一早就把對自己的關照與福祉優先放在第一位，就能為我們具有生產性而充實的一天做好準備。儘管培養良好的晨間習慣需要努力及承諾，但卻非常值得，因為它將帶來充實而有意義的生活。

The way we start our day can set the tone for the rest of the day, and our morning routine plays a crucial role in determining our overall sense of well-being and purpose. The idea that morning routine determines the whole day speaks to the importance of developing healthy habits and routines that support our physical, emotional, and spiritual well-being.

Many successful people credit their morning routines with setting the stage for their productivity and success. For example, many entrepreneurs and business leaders make a point of waking up early and dedicating the first few hours of their day to exercise, meditation, or other forms of self-care. By prioritizing their well-being and self-care first thing in the morning, they are better able to focus on their work and achieve their goals throughout the day.

Developing a healthy morning routine is not only benefi-cial for achieving professional success but also for supporting overall mental and physical health. Many experts recommend starting the day with physical exercise, as it can help to boost mood, energy levels, and overall sense of well-being. Other popular morning routine activities include journaling, meditation, reading, or engaging in creative hobbies that bring joy and fulfillment.

The specific elements of a healthy morning routine will vary depending on individual needs and preferences. However, there are several common elements that tend to be associated with successful and fulfilling mornings. These include waking up at the same time every day, avoiding electronic devices first thing in the morning, drinking water or tea, engaging in physical activity, setting intentions for the day, and practicing mindfulness or gratitude.

One of the challenges of developing a healthy morning routine is finding the time and motivation to do so. For some, this may require waking up earlier than usual or making other lifestyle changes to prioritize self-care. However, the benefits of a healthy morning routine are well worth the effort, as they can lead to increased productivity, creativity, and overall well-being.

In conclusion, the idea that morning routine determines the whole day speaks to the importance of developing healthy habits and routines that support our physical, emotional, and spiritual well-being. By prioritizing self-care and well-being first thing in the morning, we can set the stage for a productive and fulfilling day. While developing a healthy morning routine may require effort and commitment, the benefits are well worth it for a fulfilling and purposeful life.

19

創造自己的幸福，
對所有人都有益處

尋找人生目標的挑戰之一，就是在自己與他人的願望與需求之間取得平衡。從一方面來說，為了能夠活得充實，優先考量自己的快樂與幸福很重要。但從另一方面來說，我們也有責任去考慮周遭人的需求與福祉。

關於「只要不傷害他人、就以自己的幸福為重，將對所有人都有益」的想法，明確點出了一件事情的重要性，那就是要去找出個人與集體需求之間的良好平衡。因為當我們把自己的快樂幸福擺在優先，也比較能對別人付出，並對社會做出積極貢獻。

許多人誤以為優先考量自己的幸福是自私或自戀的表現。然而，照顧自己不僅是個人幸福所需，也對其他人有益。因為當我們感到快樂和滿足時，就比較可能擁有正面的人際關係、從事有效的工作，並對社會做出正向貢獻。

要記住，**優先考量自己的快樂幸福並不代表忽略他人的需求，相反的，它意味著在照顧自己和照顧他人之間找到一個健康的平衡。**為了達到真正的快樂和滿足，我們就必須擁有正面的人際關係，以及一種與他人的連結感。

而找到這個平衡的挑戰之一，就是學習如何有效地向周圍的人傳達我們的需求與渴望。我們必須學會設定界限、主張自己的需要，同時不忽略他人的需求。這可能會是一項困難的任務，但對於找到個人與集體的良好平衡來說，它非常重要。

另一個找到這個平衡的基本要素則是培養對他人的同理心和同情心。透過理解周遭人們的需求和渴望，我們將更能以一種對大家都有利的方式，來駕馭自己的需求和渴望。我們也必須願意為了團體利益而做出妥協和犧牲，但同時仍能把自己的幸福快樂放在優先。

總之，「只要不傷害他人、就以自己的幸福為重，將對所有人都有益」的這個想法，強調了找到個人與集體福祉之間良好平衡的重要性。透過優先考慮自己的快樂幸福，我們將更能為他人朝著想，並積極貢獻社會。然而，我們也必須願意設定界限、有效溝通，並對身邊的人表現出同理心與同情心。找到這個平衡可能很具挑戰性，但為了活出充實而有意義的生命，它必不可少。

One of the key challenges in finding purpose in life is balancing our own desires and needs with those of others. On the one hand, it's important to prioritize our own happiness and well-being in order to live a fulfilling life. On the other hand, we also have a responsibility to consider the needs and well-being of those around us.

The idea that, as long as it does not harm others, focusing on one's happiness and putting it first benefits everyone speaks to the importance of finding a healthy balance between individual and collective needs. When we prioritize our own happiness and well-being, we are better able to show up for others and contribute positively to society.

Many people mistakenly believe that prioritizing their own happiness is selfish or narcissistic. However, taking care of oneself is not only necessary for individual well-being but also for the benefit of others. When we are happy and fulfilled, we are more likely to have positive relationships, engage in productive work, and contribute positively to society.

It's important to note that the idea of prioritizing one's

happiness and well-being does not mean neglecting the needs of others. Rather, it means finding a healthy balance between self-care and caring for others. In order to be truly happy and fulfilled, we must have positive relationships and a sense of connection to others.

One of the challenges of finding this balance is learning how to communicate our needs and desires effectively to those around us. We must learn to set boundaries and assert our needs without neglecting the needs of others. This can be a difficult task, but it is essential for finding a healthy balance between individual and collective well-being.

Another essential aspect of finding this balance is developing empathy and compassion for others. By understanding the needs and desires of those around us, we can better navigate our own desires and needs in a way that benefits everyone. We must also be willing to compromise and make sacrifices for the benefit of the group, while still prioritizing our own happiness and well-being.

In conclusion, the idea that, as long as it does not harm

others, focusing on one's happiness and putting it first benefits everyone speaks to the importance of finding a healthy balance between individual and collective well-being. By prioritizing our own happiness and well-being, we can show up for others and contribute positively to society. However, we must also be willing to set boundaries, communicate effectively, and practice empathy and compassion for those around us. Finding this balance can be challenging, but it is essential for living a fulfilling and purposeful life.

20

即便缺乏某些事物，也不影響我們過快樂而滿足的生活

對於某些事物的缺乏，會左右一個人的行為模式、傾向、追求和目標。至於跨越這種匱乏感、進而創造充實的生活，也會充滿難度。然而，即便要面對種種缺乏的感覺，我們還是有可能去發展出有助於提升幸福感與滿足感的習慣及日常活動。

「在缺乏某些東西的情況下也能過得幸福」的關鍵之一，就是專注於感恩。當感覺缺少某些事物時，要把焦點放在你所有的東西上面，可能會很難。但練習感謝能夠幫助轉移你的觀點，並且提升正向情緒。所以請從想一些能

讓你覺得感謝的事情來開始每一天，例如你的健康，你的人際關係，你的家庭。

認真照顧自己，則是在缺乏某些事物的情況下也能過得幸福的另一個要點。因為當你把照顧自己放在優先，也會比較能夠為他人著想，並對社會做出積極貢獻。而所謂的照顧自己則可能包括睡眠充足、飲食健康、運動規律，或是參加能為你帶來快樂滿足的活動。

找到人生目標也是促進幸福和滿足感的重要因素。儘管確定自己的目標可能需要時間，但還是要去想想自己喜歡做什麼、擅長什麼以及重視什麼。並且要去思考可以如何運用自己的優點和價值，去對社會做出積極貢獻。

還有一點很重要，就是讓自己身邊圍繞積極正向、能提升並支持你的人。因為消極負面的人會帶來失望，並讓專注於積極充實的生活變得困難。所以要去找出那些能鼓勵你、與你擁有共同價值觀的人，並與他們建立積極正向的關係。

此外，學習管理壓力與焦慮也對提升幸福與滿足感有所幫助。所以要去找出對你有用的壓力管理方式，例如靜

坐冥想、深呼吸，或是運動。當你覺得不知所措或非常焦慮時，就停下來喘口氣，去做一件能為你帶來快樂的事，例如閱讀，或是親近自然。

總之，**即使缺乏某些事物也能過得幸福，需要去發展一些能夠促進生產力與滿足感的習慣與日常活動**。藉由練習感恩、認真照顧自己、找到人生目標的意識、讓自己身邊充滿正向的人，並且管理壓力及焦慮，你就能活得充實滿足，即便要與缺乏感共處。請記住，找到目標與幸福需要時間與努力，但只要心態與方法正確，就一定能實現。

Lack of something creates patterns and tendencies, pursuits, and purposes of behavior. It can be challenging to move past the feeling of lack and to create a fulfilling life. However, it is possible to develop habits and routines that promote happiness and fulfillment, even when dealing with feelings of lack.

One of the keys to living a happy life despite a lack of something is to focus on gratitude. While it may be challenging to focus on what you have when you feel like something is missing, practicing gratitude can help to shift your perspective and promote positive emotions. Begin each day by thinking of a few things you are grateful for, such as your health, your relationships, or your home.

Another important aspect of living a happy life despite a lack of something is to focus on self-care. When you prioritize taking care of yourself, you are better able to show up for others and contribute positively to society. This could mean getting enough sleep, eating healthy, exercising, and engaging in activities that bring you joy and fulfillment.

Finding a sense of purpose can also be essential in promoting happiness and fulfillment. While it may take time to identify your purpose, think about what you enjoy doing, what you are good at, and what you value. Consider how you can use your strengths and values to contribute positively to society.

It is also important to surround yourself with positive people who uplift and support you. Negative people can bring you down and make it more difficult to focus on positivity and fulfillment. Seek out positive relationships with people who encourage you and share your values.

Additionally, learning to manage stress and anxiety can be helpful in promoting happiness and fulfillment. Find ways to manage stress that work for you, such as meditation, deep breathing, or exercise. When you feel overwhelmed or anxious, take a break and engage in an activity that brings you joy, such as reading or spending time in nature.

In conclusion, living a happy life despite a lack of something requires developing habits and routines that promote positivity and fulfillment. By practicing gratitude, focusing on self-care, finding a sense of purpose, surrounding yourself with positive people, and managing stress and anxiety, you can live a fulfilling life even when dealing with feelings of lack. Remember that finding purpose and happiness takes time and effort, but it is achievable with the right mindset and approach.

21

最幸福的時刻就是「現在」

　　「現在就是最幸福的時刻」是一個重要的觀念。因為許多人會花很多時間沉湎過去或擔憂未來，以至於產生後悔、焦慮、疑惑等種種感覺。然而，透過專注於當下，並從生活中的簡單事物找到快樂，我們就能活得更充實、更幸福。

　　「練習覺察」是在當下找到快樂的重要關鍵。覺察（亦即「正念」）是一種全神貫注於此時此刻的練習，不帶任何判斷或分心。藉由專注於現在，我們就能對周遭世界發展出一種更強大的感謝與珍惜意識。

另一個在當下找到快樂的重要方法，則是學習放下過去。雖然我們過往的經歷會塑造出我們今天的樣貌，但很重要的是，不要沉溺在過去的錯誤或負面經驗之中。藉由放下過去，我們才能聚焦現在，進而創造出一個更充實的生活。

還有一件事很重要，就是要知道「幸福並非取決於外在環境」。儘管物質上的擁有、事業上的成功以及人際關係能夠帶來喜悅與滿足，但真正的幸福來自內在。所以無論外在環境如何，只要能夠培養一種積極的心態，並且專注現在，我們就能找到幸福與滿足。

從生活中的簡單事物找到喜樂，也是活在當下的重要面向。透過去欣賞自然的美、花時間跟所愛的人相處，或是投入於具創造力的嗜好之中，我們就能在日常生活中找到喜悅與滿足。

活在當下的挑戰之一，就是學習在「計畫與準備未來」及「專注與覺察現在」的需求之間取得平衡。因為<u>儘管計畫未來很重要，但聚焦當下並找出此時此刻的喜悅與滿足也很重要。</u>

總之，當談到尋找人生的目的與意義時，「最幸福的時候就是現在」的想法是一個不可或缺的概念。透過練習覺察、放下過去、專注於內在的幸福源頭、找到生活中簡單事物的喜悅，並且在計劃未來與聚焦當下之間取得平衡，我們就能活得更充實、更快樂。請牢記，幸福是一趟旅程，不是一個終點，而找到此時此刻的目標與滿足感，需要練習與實踐。

The idea that the happiest time is now is an essential concept. Many people spend a great deal of time dwelling on the past or worrying about the future, leading to feelings of regret, anxiety, and uncertainty. However, by focusing on the present moment and finding joy in the simple things in life, we can live more fully and happily.

One of the keys to finding happiness in the present moment is practicing mindfulness. Mindfulness is the practice of being fully present in the moment, without judgment or distraction. By focusing on the present moment, we can develop a greater sense of gratitude and appreciation for the world around us.

Another important aspect of finding happiness in the present moment is learning to let go of the past. While our past experiences can shape who we are today, it is important not to dwell on past mistakes or negative experiences. By letting go of the past, we can focus on the present moment and create a more fulfilling life.

It is also important to recognize that happiness is not

dependent on external circumstances. While material possessions, career success, and relationships can bring joy and fulfillment, true happiness comes from within. By cultivating a positive mindset and focusing on the present moment, we can find happiness and fulfillment regardless of our external circumstances.

Finding joy in the simple things in life is another important aspect of living in the present moment. By taking time to appreciate the beauty of nature, spending time with loved ones, or engaging in creative hobbies, we can find joy and fulfillment in our daily lives.

One of the challenges of living in the present moment is learning to balance the need for planning and preparation with the need for presence and mindfulness. While it is important to plan for the future, it is also important to focus on the present moment and find joy and fulfillment in the here and now.

In conclusion, the idea that the happiest time is now is an essential concept when it comes to finding purpose and meaning in life. By practicing mindfulness, letting go of the past, focusing on internal sources of happiness, finding joy in the simple things in life, and balancing planning with presence, we can live more fully and happily. Remember that happiness is a journey, not a destination, and finding purpose and fulfillment in the present moment requires practice and commitment.

22

生命不是被動承受，
而是神秘的冒險

....

　　生命並非只是承受，它本身就是個謎、是場冒險。但很多人渡過他們人生的方式就只是馬馬虎虎、得過且過，並沒有真正擁抱生命帶來的神秘與刺激。而透過聚焦當下、把生命當作一場發現之旅去靠近，我們才能活得更充實、更快樂。

　　活得開心的關鍵之一，就是帶著好奇心與驚奇感來對面對每一天。比起單單就只是忍耐過日子，更應該要把它視為一種探索與學習的機會來對應。要去擁抱生命中的神秘與刺激，每天都充滿期待與參與感。

對於新的經驗與機會抱持開放性，則是生活快樂的另一個重要因素。**生命充滿各種驚喜與意想不到的轉折，所以對每個新體驗帶來的可能性都要保持開放的態度。**去接受新的挑戰與機會，並帶著好奇心與求知慾去面對。

要知道，幸福不是一個終點站，而是一整趟旅行。所以不要只是把焦點放在達到特定的目標或結果，而是應該專注當下，並且去找出旅程本身的喜悅。要接受生命中的高低起伏，並把每個經驗視為成長與學習的機會。

培養積極的心態，則是生活幸福的另一個要點。要專注在你生活中的積極面向，而不是沉浸在負面想法或經驗之中。要去培養出一種對於周遭世界感謝與欣賞的意識，並用充滿樂觀與希望的態度面對每一天。

活出快樂的挑戰之一，就是在「結構化與例行公事」以及「隨性與冒險」的需求上取得平衡。儘管結構化與例行公事可以帶來穩定感與安全感，但它們也可能變成單調而乏味。透過接受隨性與冒險，我們才能為日常生活注入一種期待與喜悅的感受。

總而言之，對於尋找人生目標與意義來說，「生活並非忍受，而是神祕與冒險」的想法是一個重要概念。藉由接受生命中的神祕與冒險、以好奇心與驚奇感面對每一天、對新的經驗與機會保持開放性、聚焦於旅程本身而非終點、培養積極心態，並且在結構性與隨性之間取得平衡，我們就能活得更加充實而快樂。要記住，尋找人生目標與幸福是一趟旅行，而不是一個目的地。而實現生活的關鍵，就是去擁抱生命中的種種神祕與冒險。

Life is not about enduring, but a mystery and adventure in itself, many people spend their lives simply going through the motions, without truly embracing the mystery and adventure that life has to offer. However, by focusing on the present moment and approaching life as a journey of discovery, we can live more fully and happily.

One of the keys to living a happy life is to approach each day with a sense of curiosity and wonder. Rather than simply enduring the day, approach it as an opportunity to explore and learn. Embrace the mystery and adventure of life, and approach each day with a sense of excitement and anticipation.

Another important aspect of living a happy life is to be open to new experiences and opportunities. Life is full of surprises and unexpected twists and turns, and it is important to be open to the possibilities that each new experience brings. Embrace new challenges and opportunities, and approach them with a sense of curiosity and wonder.

It is also important to recognize that happiness is not a destination, but a journey. Rather than focusing on achieving specific goals or outcomes, focus on the present moment and finding joy in the journey itself. Embrace the ups and downs of life, and approach each experience as an opportunity to learn and grow.

Developing a positive mindset is another essential aspect of living a happy life. Focus on the positive aspects of your life, rather than dwelling on negative thoughts or experiences. Cultivate a sense of gratitude and appreciation for the world around you, and approach each day with a sense of optimism and hope.

One of the challenges of living a happy life is learning to balance the need for structure and routine with the need for spontaneity and adventure. While structure and routine can provide a sense of stability and security, they can also become monotonous and dull. By embracing spontaneity and adventure, we can inject a sense of excitement and joy into our daily lives.

In conclusion, the idea that life is not about enduring, but a mystery and adventure in itself is an essential concept when it comes to finding purpose and meaning in life. By embracing the mystery and adventure of life, approaching each day with a sense of curiosity and wonder, being open to new experiences and opportunities, focusing on the journey rather than the destination, developing a positive mindset, and balancing structure with spontaneity, we can live more fully and happily. Remember that finding purpose and happiness is a journey, not a destination, and that the key to a fulfilling life is embracing the mystery and adventure of life.

Chpater 4.
接受人生中不變的真理

此圖為AI以書名、目錄和主題為指令而繪製的封面初稿之一。

第四章聚焦探討「在人生不變的真理中尋找方向」。具體來說，我們要討論的是：接受死亡的必然性並且學習活在當下，將有助於確認我們的人生目標與方向。

有一個要去思考的關鍵點，就是我們都必須面對「人總有一天會死」的事實。儘管這可能會讓人一想起來就很不安，但接受這個事實能幫助我們更加完全的活在當下。因為透過認知到人在世界上活著的時間有限，我們就會開始把對我們真正重要的事物放在優先，並且活得更有目標意識。

很重要的一點是，真正的心靈平靜只存於現在。雖然我們很自然地會去反思過去與計劃未來，但沉溺於這些可能會讓我們錯過此時此刻所擁有的財富。透過學習活在當下，我們可以培養出更大的覺察與感知，進而在我們的日常生活體驗中找到更深層的意義與目標。

為了培養這種當下的覺知，就要投入時間去從客觀的角度來抓住現在。這個意思是，要去學習不帶判斷或執著地觀察我們的思想、情緒及感覺，並且對於我們周遭的世界更加敏銳。正念練習，例如冥想，可以成為這個過程中有用的工具，幫助我們培養出更強大的覺察力與存在感。

　　另一個找到人生方向的重要方法，就是要去挑戰我們向來認為理所當然的事。因為我們很容易陷入來自文化或社會經驗而產生的思想與行為模式，而非根據我們自己的個人價值觀或願望行事。藉由質疑那些理所當然的設想，我們才能開始去找出自己真正的熱情所在與優先順序，並且按照我們最深的目標意識來規劃進程。

　　最後一點則是要記住，我們並不需要什麼都做。雖然要達到特定目標或里程碑自然會讓人感到壓力，但終究是由我們自己來定義人生中的成功與目標究竟是什麼。藉由學習放下外部期望，聽取自己的內在指引，我們才能開創一種真正覺得滿足而有意義的生活。

　　總之，第四章聚焦於接受生命中不變的真理，包括死亡的必然性，可以幫助我們在生活中找到方向和目標。透過學習活在當下，挑戰我們認為理所當然的想法，並且聆

聽自己內在的導引，我們就能制定出符合自己最深層價值
觀與願望的計劃。

Chapter 4 focused on the theme of finding direction
in the unchanging truth of life. Specifically, we are exploring
the idea that accepting the inevitability of death and learning
to live in the present moment can help us to identify our
purpose and direction in life.

One of the key points to consider is that we must all
face the fact that we will one day die. While this may be an
uncomfortable truth to contemplate, accepting it can help
us to live more fully in the present moment. By recognizing
that our time on earth is limited, we can begin to prioritize the
things that truly matter to us, and live with a greater sense of
purpose and intention.

The important point is that the only true peace of mind
lies in the present moment. While it's natural to reflect on the
past and plan for the future, dwelling on these things can

cause us to miss out on the richness of the present moment. By learning to live in the here and now, we can cultivate a greater sense of mindfulness and awareness, and find deeper meaning and purpose in our daily experiences.

In order to cultivate this present-moment awareness, it's important to invest time in grasping the present from an objective point of view. This means learning to observe our thoughts, emotions, and sensations without judgment or attachment, and becoming more attuned to the world around us. Mindfulness practices such as meditation can be useful tools in this process, helping us to cultivate greater awareness and presence.

Another important strategy for finding direction in life is to challenge the assumptions that we have taken for granted. It's easy to fall into patterns of thought and behavior that are based on cultural or societal expectations, rather than our own individual values and desires. By questioning these assumptions, we can begin to uncover our true passions and priorities, and chart a course that aligns with our deepest sense of purpose.

Finally, it's important to remember that we don't have to do anything. While it's natural to feel pressure to achieve certain goals or milestones, it's ultimately up to us to define what success and purpose mean in our own lives. By learning to let go of external expectations and tune into our own inner guidance, we can create a life that feels truly fulfilling and meaningful.

In summary, Chapter 4 focused on the idea that accepting the unchanging truth of life, including the inevitability of death, can help us to find direction and purpose in life. By learning to live in the present moment, challenging our assumptions, and tuning into our own inner guidance, we can chart a course that aligns with our deepest values and desires.

23

總有一天會死，
所以要做自己的生命設計師

‧‧‧‧‧‧‧‧‧‧‧‧‧‧‧‧‧‧‧‧‧‧‧‧‧‧‧‧‧‧‧‧‧‧‧‧‧‧

「死亡不可避免」是生命的一個基本事實。而接受這個事實，對於如何能建構出有意義與目標的生活來說，則會是一個強而有力的工具。這裡提供一些技術，讓你可以在「必定會死」的前提下做自己的生命設計師：

1.澄清你的價值觀：清楚知道對自己來說什麼最重要，能有助於你做出符合目標的選擇。要去問問自己，<u>在生命中你會把哪些價值觀放在優先</u>。舉例來說，可能包括：家庭、社群、靈性、冒險、創造力，或是個人成長。

2.設定有意義的目標：當你對自己的價值觀有清楚認知，就可以設定出與它們相符合的目標。所以要去思考<u>自己想在生命中成就什麼，又想留下什麼遺產</u>。無論是養家、創業、為社群做出改變，或是追求一種熱情，只要具有目標意識，就能幫助你保持動力與專注。

3.活在當下：雖然對於未來要有目標與計劃很重要，但好好活在現在也同樣重要。也因此，要去<u>珍惜每天生活中的微小喜悅，並且培養正念與感謝</u>。請記住，生命可貴、稍縱即逝，所以要好好善用每一刻。

4.面對恐懼：對於死亡的畏懼可能成為強大的動力，也可能會是造成停頓的驅力。藉由<u>承認並面對恐懼，你將學會更加完全的擁抱生命</u>。所以要問問自己害怕什麼以及為什麼害怕，並想想可以採取哪些行動去克服那些恐懼。

5.實踐自我反思：<u>定期反省生活可以幫助你保持與自己的目標及價值觀連結。</u>所以，要撥出一些時間去寫日誌、冥想，或只是安靜坐下來回想自己經歷過的事。然後認真思考什麼是自己已經學到的、什麼又是你覺得感謝的，以及什麼是你依然希望達成的。

即便面對生命的有限性，但只要把這些技巧納入生活之中，就能設計出具有目標與意義的人生。請記住，死亡是生命中很自然的一個部分，而透過活得有目標、有意識，你將能在離世之後留下正向遺產，並且持續長存。

The inevitability of death is a fundamental truth of life. Accepting this fact can be a powerful tool in designing a meaningful and purposeful life. Here are some techniques for designing a life based on the certainty of death:

1.Clarify your values: Knowing what matters most to you can help you make choices that align with your purpose. Ask yourself what values you want to prioritize in your life. Some examples might include family, community, spirituality, adventure, creativity, or personal growth.

2.Set meaningful goals: When you have a clear sense of your values, you can set goals that align with them. Think about what you want to accomplish in your life and what legacy you want to leave behind. Whether it's raising a family, building a business, making a difference in your community, or pursuing a passion, having a sense of purpose can help you stay motivated and focused.

3.Live in the present: While it's important to have goals and plans for the future, it's equally important to live in the present moment. Appreciate the small joys in your daily life, and cultivate mindfulness and gratitude. Remember that life is precious and fleeting, and make the most of every moment.

4.Face your fears: The fear of death can be a powerful motivator or a paralyzing force. By acknowledging and facing your fears, you can learn to embrace life more fully. Ask yourself what you're afraid of and why, and consider what steps you can take to overcome those fears.

5.Practice self-reflection: Regularly reflecting on your life can help you stay connected to your purpose and values. Set aside time to journal, meditate, or simply sit in silence and reflect on your experiences. Consider what you've learned, what you're grateful for, and what you still hope to achieve.

Incorporating these techniques into your life can help you design a purposeful and meaningful life, even in the face of mortality. Remember that death is a natural part of life, and that by living with purpose and intention, you can leave a positive legacy that will endure long after you're gone.

24

內心的平靜無關過去
與未來，只存於現在

　　找到內心的平靜是許多人的共同目標，然而它可能很難達到。會這樣的原因之一，是因為我們經常把焦點放在過去或未來，而不是好好活在現在。下面提供一些可藉由務實活在當下而找到內心平靜的技巧：

　　1.練習覺察： 覺察（意即「正念」）是一種不帶任何判斷、只認真關注現在的實踐。它能幫助你保持對當下的專心，而不會被對過去的後悔或對未來的憂慮帶走。試著去練習覺察，透過冥想、深呼吸，或是只專注於你對此時此刻的各種感覺。

2.放下過去：緊緊抓著從前的傷害、悔恨或是錯誤不放，會讓你現在不能找到內心的平靜。儘管承認過去並從中學習很重要，但沉溺其中會傷害你的幸福。所以要練習原諒，無論對他人或是自己，並且要聚焦於當下，而不要再耽溺於過往。

3.培養感謝心：感謝是一個強大的工具，有助於尋找此刻內心的平靜。透過把焦點放在現在所感謝的事物上，你就能把注意力從對於未來的憂慮、對於過去的悔恨之中轉移開來。試著寫下感謝日記，或者單純只是每天花幾分鐘去回想什麼事情讓你覺得感謝。

4.有意識地去生活：這是指在生活中要有意識的去做出與你價值觀與目標相符的種種決定。透過專注於現在想要達成的事物，你就能避免因為憂慮未來或悔恨過去而分心。為自己設定目標並且採取行動，一步一步慢慢來。

5.練習自我關照：現在好好照顧自己就可以幫助你找到內心的平靜。無論是睡得充足、吃得營養，還是參加能讓你開心的活動，只要把照顧自己放在優先，就能讓你腳踏實地，感到更加安心自在。

透過聚焦於現在，即便是在混亂或不確定的情況下，你仍然可以找到內心的平靜。請記住，過去已經過去，未來還沒有到來，而現在卻永遠是你隨手可得的。所以**要練習覺察、放掉過去、培養感謝心、有意識地去生活，並且練習照顧自己，這樣就能活得踏實，找到內心的平靜。**

Finding peace of mind is a common goal for many people, yet it can be elusive. One reason for this is that we often focus on the past or the future, rather than living in the present moment. Here are some techniques for finding peace of mind by staying grounded in the present:

1. Practice mindfulness: Mindfulness is the practice of paying attention to the present moment without judgment. It can help you stay focused on the here and now, rather than getting caught up in regrets about the past or worries about the future. Try practicing mindfulness through meditation, deep breathing, or simply paying attention to your senses in the present moment.

2. Let go of the past: Holding onto past hurts, regrets, or mistakes can prevent you from finding peace in the present. While it's important to acknowledge and learn from the past, dwelling on it can be detrimental to your well-being. Practice forgiveness, both for others and for yourself, and focus on the present moment rather than dwelling on the past.

3. Cultivate gratitude: Gratitude is a powerful tool for

finding peace of mind in the present. By focusing on what you're grateful for in the present moment, you can shift your attention away from worries about the future or regrets about the past. Try keeping a gratitude journal or simply taking a few minutes each day to reflect on what you're grateful for.

4. Live with intention: Living with intention means making conscious choices that align with your values and goals. By focusing on what you want to achieve in the present moment, you can avoid getting distracted by worries about the future or regrets about the past. Set goals for yourself and take action towards them, one step at a time.

5. Practice self-care: Taking care of yourself in the present moment can help you find peace of mind. Whether it's getting enough sleep, eating nourishing food, or engaging in activities that bring you joy, prioritizing self-care can help you stay grounded in the present and feel more at ease.

By staying focused on the present moment, you can find peace of mind even in the midst of chaos or uncertainty. Remember that the past is gone and the future is not yet here, but the present moment is always available to you. Practice mindfulness, let go of the past, cultivate gratitude, live with intention, and practice self-care to stay grounded in the present and find peace of mind.

投入時間，
學習以客觀角度來看待世界

尋找人生的目標和意義，需要我們對自己和周遭世界有深刻的理解。而獲得這種理解的方式之一，就是投入時間，去用客觀的角度來掌握現在。下面是這樣做的一些技巧：

自我意識是一種客觀觀察和了解自己想法、感覺與行為舉止的能力。透過發展自我意識，你就能對自己以及你的動力來源獲得更深的理解。試著去寫日記、接受性格評估，或者只是簡單的專注於你一整天下來的想法與感受。

同理心是一種了解並分享他人感受的能力。藉由培養同理心，你就能對周遭世界產生比較客觀的見解。試著站在其他人的立場，主動聆聽，並且找出共同點。

人都會有許多可能蒙蔽判斷的假想與偏見，導致我們無法客觀看待這個世界。藉由挑戰你的臆測並找出不一樣的見解，你就能對世界有更細緻入微的認知。可以試試多去閱讀不同觀點的書籍文章，或多去跟具有不同見解的人進行具思考性的對話。

批判性思考是一種客觀分析與評估資訊的能力。透過開發你的批判性思考技巧，你就能做出更明智的決定，並且更客觀的了解世界。試著多去提出問題、評估證據，並思考替代性的解釋。

覺察是一種不帶任何判斷、專心關注當下的練習。藉由練習覺察，你將能培養出對於自己的想法與感受更加客觀的見解。試著去冥想、深呼吸，或者只是簡單地把注意力放在你現在的感覺。

透過花時間去從客觀角度來掌握現在，你可以對自己與周遭世界有更深刻的了解。**練習自我意識、培養同理**

心、挑戰你先入為主的設想、進行批判性思考，並且練習覺察，就能開發出較為客觀的見解。要記住，客觀並不是要你毫無感情或漠不關心。相反的，它代表著要能夠去觀察並理解自己以及他人的想法與感受，而不會深陷其中受到束縛。

Finding purpose and meaning in life requires a deep understanding of ourselves and the world around us. One way to gain this understanding is by investing time in grasping the present from an objective point of view. Here are some techniques for doing so:

Self-awareness is the ability to objectively observe and understand your thoughts, feelings, and behaviors. By developing self-awareness, you can gain a deeper understanding of yourself and your motivations. Try journaling, taking personality assessments, or simply paying attention to your thoughts and feelings throughout the day.

Empathy is the ability to understand and share the feelings of others. By cultivating empathy, you can gain a more objective perspective on the world around you. Try putting yourself in other people's shoes, listening actively, and looking for common ground.

We all have assumptions and biases that can cloud our judgment and prevent us from seeing the world objectively. By challenging your assumptions and seeking out different perspectives, you can gain a more nuanced understanding of the world. Try reading books or articles from different viewpoints, or engaging in thoughtful conversations with people who have different perspectives.

Critical thinking is the ability to objectively analyze and evaluate information. By developing your critical thinking skills, you can make more informed decisions and understand the world more objectively. Try asking questions, evaluating evidence, and considering alternative explanations.

Mindfulness is the practice of paying attention to the present moment without judgment. By practicing mindfulness, you can develop a more objective perspective on your thoughts and emotions. Try meditating, deep breathing, or simply paying attention to your senses in the present moment.

By investing time in grasping the present from an objective point of view, you can gain a deeper understanding of yourself and the world around you. Practice self-awareness, cultivate empathy, challenge your assumptions, engage in critical thinking, and practice mindfulness to develop a more objective perspective. Remember that objectivity doesn't mean you have to be emotionless or detached. Instead, it means being able to observe and understand your thoughts and feelings, as well as those of others, without getting caught up in them.

26

要對向來被視為
理所當然的價值觀提出質疑

我們的標準會塑造出我們的信念、價值觀與行動，並且往往在我們不自覺的情況下發生。去挑戰向來認為理所當然的標準，將有助我們對自己與周遭世界有更深的理解。下面是這樣做的一些方法：

首先，就從確認那些奠定自己信念與行動的價值觀開始。你可以問問自己為什麼相信自己的所作所為，以及，在那些信念背後的假設是什麼。舉例來說，你可能認為成功是由財富與地位所定義，也可能認為幸福是來自於外在的資源。

一旦確定了你的價值觀，就要開始提出質疑。問問自己它們是否基於事實，或單純只是個人信念。想想看有什麼依據是支持或反對你的假設，並且尋找替代性的想法。

尋求不同觀點：讓自己接觸不一樣的觀點，能有助於挑戰自己的假設。所以要去找出那些跟自己看法不同的觀點，無論透過閱讀、對話，或是其他形式的媒介。

嘗試新的作為：嘗試新的行為與體驗能對挑戰自己的假設有所幫助。舉例來說，如果你認為自己需要很多錢才會快樂，那就試著在一段時間內生活得簡樸一點，看看這樣做會怎麼影響你的快樂。

接受不確定性：挑戰自己的假設有時可能會讓人感到不舒服甚至覺得害怕。但是要去接受這種不確定性，並且認知到挑戰自己的假設是一個持續的過程，而不是一次性的事件。

藉由挑戰我們向來認為理所當然的假設，就能對自己與周遭世界有更深入的了解。所以要去確認假設、質疑它們、尋求多元觀點、嘗試新的作為，並且接受不確定性來挑戰自己的假設。請記住，**挑戰假設並不代表要放棄你的**

價值觀或信念，而是要不斷地去質疑它們，並且讓它們更加完善。

Our standards shape our beliefs, values, and actions, often without us even realizing it. Challenging the standards we take for granted can help us gain a deeper understanding of ourselves and the world around us. Here are some techniques for doing so:

Start by identifying the values that underlie your beliefs and actions. Ask yourself why you believe what you do, and what assumptions are behind those beliefs. For example, you might assume that success is defined by wealth and status, or that happiness comes from external sources.

Once you've identified your values, start questioning them. Ask yourself whether they are based on facts or simply beliefs. Consider the evidence for and against your assumptions, and look for alternative perspectives.

Seek out diverse perspectives: Exposing yourself to different perspectives can help you challenge your assumptions. Seek out viewpoints that are different from your own, whether through reading, conversation, or other forms of media.

Experiment with new behaviors: Trying out new behaviors and experiences can help you challenge your assumptions. For example, if you assume that you need a lot of money to be happy, try living more simply for a period of time and see how it affects your happiness.

Embrace uncertainty: Challenging your assumptions can be uncomfortable and even scary at times. Embrace the uncertainty and recognize that challenging your assumptions is an ongoing process, not a one-time event.

By challenging the assumptions we take for granted, we can gain a deeper understanding of ourselves and the world around us. Identify your assumptions, question them, seek out diverse perspectives, experiment with new behaviors, and embrace uncertainty to challenge your assumptions. Remember that challenging your assumptions doesn't mean abandoning your values or beliefs, but rather questioning them and refining them over time.

27

不是每件事都非做不可

只要提到尋找人生目標，通常就會有很大的壓力要去做些什麼事情。因為我們會被告知要定下目標、追求熱情、好好利用時間。但是，如果你並不覺得有被特定的熱情驅使、也對想達成的目標沒有什麼明確想法呢？如果你就是滿足於現狀，而且不覺得有改變任何事物的需要呢？

不同於一般看法，其實對於完成特定事物沒有強烈熱情一點也沒有關係。因為並不是每個人都需要成為優等生，也並不是每個人都需要有明確目標才能快樂。有時候，只是單純活著並享受當中的種種微小事物就已足夠。

很重要的是要知道，作為一個人的價值並不是由成就來決定。**你很珍貴，單純就只因為你存在，你並不需要去做任何事來證明自己的價值。**事實上，不斷努力達到更多只會令人精疲力竭，而且終究還是覺得不滿。

話雖如此，但去**辨別出自己究竟是沒有特定目標，或者就只是感覺被卡住或不滿足，這很重要。如果發現自己毫無目標或缺乏動力，那就很值得去探討為什麼會這樣。**你之所以沒有去追求自己的熱情所在，也許是因為你還不知道它們是什麼，也可能是因為害怕失敗。又或者，你可能被困在一種不符合自己價值觀或沒有目標感的工作或生活模式之中。

如果真的覺得自己缺乏方向，還是有很多方法可以找到滿足感，而不一定要去追求一個特定的目標。下面是一些建議：

與他人建立關係：人際關係會是獲得滿足感與意義的重要來源。所以要去聯繫朋友及家人，也可以考慮去做義工或是參加社團。

投入嗜好活動：培養興趣和嗜好能帶來目標意識與愉

悅感受，即便它們不會帶來任何具體的成就。

練習覺察：對於所處的當下保持覺知與意識，能有助於你在日常體驗中找到滿足與意義。

幫助他人：為他人的福祉做出貢獻，能夠帶來一種目標意識與對自己滿意的感覺。

終究，決定什麼可以帶來滿足感和人生意義，取決於每個人自己。對於有些人來說，可能是要去追求特定的目標或熱情，但對其他人來說，則可能只是簡單享受當下。關鍵在於要知道，尋找人生目標並沒有什麼「正確」的方法，你大可以用自己的步調去進行。

When it comes to finding purpose in life, there's often a lot of pressure to do something. We're told to set goals, pursue our passions, and make the most of our time. But what if you don't feel driven by a particular passion or have a clear idea of what you want to achieve? What if you're simply content with your current situation and don't feel the need to change anything?

Contrary to popular belief, it's perfectly okay to not have a burning desire to accomplish something specific. Not everyone needs to be an overachiever, and not everyone needs to have a clear purpose to be happy. Sometimes, simply living life and enjoying the little things can be enough.

It's important to recognize that your worth as a person is not determined by your accomplishments. You are valuable simply because you exist, and you don't need to do anything in order to prove your worth. In fact, constantly striving to achieve more can be exhausting and ultimately unfulfilling.

That being said, it's important to distinguish between not having a specific purpose and simply feeling stuck or unfulfilled. If you find yourself feeling aimless or unmotivated, it's worth exploring why that might be the case. Perhaps you're not pursuing your passions because you don't know what they are yet, or because you're afraid of failure. Alternatively, you might be stuck in a job or lifestyle that doesn't align with your values or provide a sense of purpose.

If you do feel like you're lacking direction, there are still plenty of ways to find fulfillment without necessarily pursuing a specific goal. Here are a few suggestions:

Connect with others: Relationships can be a major source of fulfillment and meaning. Reach out to friends and family, or consider volunteering or joining a club or group.

Engage in hobbies: Pursuing interests and hobbies can provide a sense of purpose and enjoyment, even if they don't lead to any specific accomplishments.

Practice mindfulness: Being present and aware in the moment can help you find contentment and meaning in everyday experiences.

Help others: Contributing to the well-being of others can provide a sense of purpose and satisfaction.

Ultimately, it's up to each individual to determine what brings them fulfillment and meaning. For some, this might mean pursuing a specific goal or passion, while for others, it might mean simply enjoying the present moment. The key is to recognize that there is no one "right" way to find purpose, and that it's okay to take things at your own pace.

Chpater 5.
覺察人生目標的根基所在

此圖為 AI 以書名、目錄和主題為指令而繪製的封面初稿之一。

尋找人生目標是一場個人的旅程，而它通常會與「去追求什麼是我們個人想要達成的」有關。雖然我們的目標意識也許有時候會被認為很自私，但它不一定是件負面的事。重要的是要有所認知，我們的目標乃是基於我們獨特的經驗與觀點，而這會是我們生命中的一股驅動力。

　　那麼，生命中真正重要的是什麼呢？這個問題的答案因人而異，但一般來說，我們的經驗、所學所知，以及與周遭人們的關係，會是生命中最重要的一些事物。所以關鍵就在於要去辨識出什麼對我們來說真正重要的，並且把它們優先放在其它會令我們分心的事物之前。

　　找到人生目標需要我們付出代價，這可能會是時間、精力，或是以犧牲的形式來付出。但我們所付出的代價，最後會值得讓我們在實現目標時獲得回報。而為了能有效率的達成目標，我們就需要在金錢、時間與熱情上取得平

衡，並且適當地投資它們。

　　成功與我們為了追求目標所付出的努力成正比。實現目標需要大量的時間與精力，而且我們需要維持這股力量繼續前行。所以應該記住，我們也許沒有辦法現在就實現所有想要的一切，但關鍵是要不斷推動自己朝向目標邁進。

　　我們行動的方式和我們所獲得的成果一樣重要。為了達到目標，我們必須採取達標的必要行動。如果不確定該採取什麼行動，那麼，去尋求建議或是讀本書來探索行動最佳方案，都是好辦法。我們也應該要記住，朝向目標的過程就跟目的地一樣重要。

　　尋找人生目標要根據我們的獨特經驗與觀點。我們可能必須付出代價，但當實現目標時，這會是值得的。對於我們的金錢、時間與精力，要能取得平衡，並且適當的投資它們以達成目標。因為成功與我們為追求目標所付出的努力成正比，而我們怎麼行動就跟結果一樣重要。要記住，朝向人生目標的過程就跟目的地同樣要緊，所以我們應該不斷保持推動自己朝向目標邁進。

Finding the purpose of life is a personal journey, and it often involves pursuing what we individually want to achieve. Our sense of purpose may sometimes be considered selfish, but it doesn't necessarily have to be a negative thing. It's important to understand that our purpose is based on our unique experiences and perspectives, and this can be a driving force in our lives.

So, what is really important in life? The answer to this question varies from person to person, but in general, our experiences, what we have learned, and our relationships with those around us are some of the most important things in life. It's crucial to identify what truly matters to us and to prioritize those things over other distractions.

Finding our purpose in life requires us to pay a price, and this could be in the form of time, effort, or sacrifice. But the price we pay is ultimately worth the reward we receive when we achieve our goals. We need to balance our money, time, and passion, and invest them properly to reach our goals effectively.

Success is proportional to the size of the strength we can muster to pursue our goals. Achieving our purpose requires a considerable amount of time and effort, and we need to sustain that strength to keep going. We should remember that we might not be able to achieve everything we want right away, but it's crucial to keep pushing ourselves towards the goal.

The way we act is as important as the result we achieve. To achieve our purpose, we must take the necessary actions to reach our goals. If we're not sure which actions to take, it's a good idea to seek advice or read a book to gain some insight into the best course of action. We should also remember that the journey towards our purpose is just as important as the destination.

Finding our purpose in life is based on our unique experiences and perspectives. We may have to pay a price, but it's worth it when we achieve our goals. We should balance our money, time, and passion, and invest them properly to reach our goals effectively. Success is proportional to the size of the strength we can muster to pursue our goals, and how we act is as important as the result. Remember that the journey towards our purpose is just as important as the destination, and we should keep pushing ourselves to reach our goals.

28

人追求的目標都是自私的，
這沒有問題

　　尋找人生目標的概念，是一個在歷史進程中不斷被廣泛討論的課題。雖然很多人認為他們的人生目標應該要無私或利他，但「人生目標就該自私」的想法，在近年來也獲得認同。這個看法認為，追求個人的幸福與滿足應該才是主要重點，而不是其他被視為更大利益的事物。

　　那些主張個人目標就是要自私的人指出，追求幸福是一種基本的人性需求。從這個觀點來看，為了造就滿足的人生，優先考慮我們個人的需要與慾望至為重要。因為藉由把焦點放在什麼能讓我們快樂，我們才能為自己創造出

一種更有意義與目標的存在。

此外，這個觀點的支持者也認為，我們對於幸福和滿足的追求最終也能造福他人。因為透過快樂和滿足感，我們可以積極影響周遭的人，甚至或許能啟發他們去找到自己的人生目標、追求自己的幸福。而這會創造出一種漣漪效應，為每個人帶來更大的幸福與滿足感。

然而，有些人也許認為，把關注點放在個人的幸福和滿足感上，會導致一種自私自利、以自我為中心的生活方式。因為他們可能相信，真正的人生目標和意義只存在於能為更大利益效勞的事物上，例如幫助他人，或是為了共同目標而努力。

雖然去對更大利益的事物做出貢獻確實重要，但並不需要在過程中犧牲我們自己的幸福與滿足。事實上，**當我們感到幸福滿足時，往往我們也才比較能幫助到其他的人。透過把自己的需要與慾望放在優先，我們也才更能照顧到周遭人的需求。**

藉由在這兩大優先考慮當中取得平衡，我們就能為自己與身邊的人創造出一種更有目標與意義的生活。

The concept of finding one's purpose in life is a topic that has been discussed extensively throughout history. While many people believe that their purpose should be something selfless or altruistic, the idea that one's purpose is just selfish has gained traction in recent years. This view suggests that the pursuit of individual happiness and fulfillment should be the primary focus, regardless of whether it serves a greater good.

Those who argue that one's purpose is just selfish often point out that the pursuit of happiness is a fundamental human need. From this perspective, it is essential to prioritize our individual needs and desires in order to lead a fulfilling life. By focusing on what makes us happy, we can create a more meaningful and purposeful existence for ourselves.

Moreover, proponents of this view argue that our pursuit of happiness and fulfillment can ultimately benefit others as well. By being happy and fulfilled, we can positively influence those around us, and perhaps even inspire them to find their own purpose and pursue their own happiness. This can create a ripple effect that can lead to greater happiness and fulfillment for everyone.

However, some may argue that a focus on individual happiness and fulfillment can lead to a selfish, self-centered existence. They may believe that true purpose and meaning can only be found by serving a greater good, such as helping others or working towards a common goal.

While it is certainly important to contribute to the greater good, it is not necessary to sacrifice our own happiness and fulfillment in the process. In fact, we are often better able to serve others when we are happy and fulfilled ourselves. By prioritizing our own needs and desires, we can better serve the needs of those around us.

By finding a balance between these two priorities, we can create a more purposeful and meaningful existence for ourselves and those around us.

29

生命中真正重要的是什麼？

對於人生目標的追尋，往往歸結到一個根本問題，那就是：生命中真正重要的是什麼？跨越文化與世代，這是一個在歷史進程中不斷被人們追問的問題。雖然這個問題難以回答，但卻是一個為了活出充實有意義的人生而值得去探索的問題。

「生命中真正重要的是什麼」之核心所在，就是價值觀的想法。價值觀是那些對我們來說最為重要的原則或信仰。它指引我們的行為、我們的決定，並且最終指引我們對於目標的意識。而我們的價值觀會受到各種不同因素的影響，例如文化、宗教、個人經驗，以及人際關係。

有些共同的價值觀是許多人高度重視的，包括家庭、愛、健康及幸福。這些價值觀往往互為相關，而且能提供一種實現生命的基礎。舉例來說，跟家人之間有一種強大的愛與連結感，會對我們全面性的幸福快樂都有助益。

然而，關於「生命中真正重要的是什麼」這個問題，可能帶有高度的主觀性。因為對於某人很重要的事物，也許對另外一個人來說並不重要。而這就是何以每個人要去反思自己的價值觀與優先順序很重要的原因。

另一個需要考慮的重要因素是人生目標的角色。儘管價值觀提供了基礎，但人生目標才是我們努力追求的總體標的。人生目標可以被視為我們存在的原因，或是行動背後的驅動力，也正是它是賦予了我們生命的意義與方向。

尋找自己的目標會是一個具有挑戰性且持續進行的過程，但它值得去追求。我們的目標會受到價值觀，以及我們的熱情、興趣與才能的影響。當我們找到一個與自己價值觀及真實自我相符的目標，就會體驗到一種滿足、如意的深刻感受。

除了價值觀與目標之外，生命中真正重要事物的另一

個面向則是人際關係。我們生活中的人會對我們的幸福與目標意識產生重大影響。去培養與家人、朋友及社群的正向關係，將能有助於帶來歸屬感與連結感。

最後，還要對外在因素的角色有所認知，例如社會壓力以及來自文化背景的期待。儘管意識到這些因素很重要，但同樣重要的是，要記得，指引我們決定與行動的，應該是我們自己的價值觀與目標。

總之，生命中真正重要的事物是一個深層的個人與主觀問題。然而，**透過反思我們的價值觀、找到自己的目標、培養正向人際關係並忠於自己，我們就能創造出充實而有意義的人生。**

The search for the purpose of life often boils down to one fundamental question: what is really important in life? This is a question that has been asked by people throughout history, across cultures and generations. It is a question that can be difficult to answer, but one that is worth exploring in order to live a fulfilling and meaningful life.

At the core of what is really important in life is the idea of values. Values are the principles or beliefs that are most important to us. They guide our behavior, our decisions, and ultimately, our sense of purpose. Our values can be influenced by a variety of factors, such as culture, religion, personal experiences, and relationships.

Some common values that many people hold dear include family, love, health, and happiness. These values are often interrelated, and they can provide a foundation for a fulfilling life. For example, a strong sense of love and connection with family members can contribute to our overall happiness and well-being.

However, the question of what is really important in

life can be highly subjective. What may be important to one person may not be important to another. This is why it is important for each individual to reflect on their own values and priorities.

Another important factor to consider is the role of purpose. While values provide a foundation, purpose is the overarching goal that we strive for. Purpose can be thought of as the reason for our existence or the driving force behind our actions. It is what gives our life meaning and direction.

Finding one's purpose can be a challenging and ongoing process, but it is one that is worth pursuing. Our purpose can be influenced by our values, as well as our passions, interests, and talents. When we find a purpose that aligns with our values and our true self, we can experience a deep sense of fulfillment and satisfaction.

In addition to values and purpose, another important aspect of what is really important in life is relationships. The people in our lives can have a significant impact on our well-being and our sense of purpose. Nurturing positive relationships with family, friends, and community can provide a sense of belonging and connection.

Finally, it is important to acknowledge the role of external factors, such as societal pressures and cultural expectations. While it is important to be aware of these factors, it is equally important to remember that our own values and purpose should guide our decisions and actions.

In summary, the question of what is really important in life is a deeply personal and subjective one. However, by reflecting on our values, finding our purpose, nurturing positive relationships, and being true to ourselves, we can create a fulfilling and meaningful life.

30

找尋目標的過程中，
必須承擔代價

· ·

　　追求人生目標和意義往往需要犧牲與努力。有一個普遍的信念，就是為了成就某些有價值的事物，人必須願意付出代價。這可能包括犧牲時間、精力，甚至是個人慾望，就為了要實現更大的目標。

　　人必須付出代價的想法，在人生許多方面都能看得出來，從人際關係到事業成功皆然。舉例來說，為了建立良好充實的人際關係，個人可能需要為了雙方利益而做出妥協與奉獻。在職場上，則可能需要投入很長時間並付諸個人犧牲，才能夠達到專業上的成就。

然而，為了實現自己的目標而付出代價可不容易。因為這會需要很大的決心、堅持和韌性。而且這也會需要一種去接受冒險並跨出舒適圈的意願。

付出代價去實現目標的關鍵因素之一，就是擁有明確的目標意識。**當個人具有強烈的目標意識，就會更加願意為了達成目標而做出犧牲。**因為目標會帶來克服障礙、面對挑戰不屈不撓的動機與推力。

另一個重要的因素是心態。**那些能夠為實現目標而付出代價的人往往擁有成長型心態，而其特徵就是相信透過努力與經驗能夠帶來學習與成長。**因為這種心態能讓個人把挑戰視為成長的機會，並且用堅持與決心來面對障礙。

同時，也要知道，為實現目標而付出代價並不是一個線性過程。一路上可能會遇到挫折、失敗以及意外的挑戰。然而，這些挑戰可以被視為成長與學習的機會。**藉由接受這些挑戰並且堅持不懈，個人將能發展出達成目標所需要的技能與韌性。**

總之，對於追求人生目標與意義來說，「必須付出代價」是一個基本概念。儘管做出犧牲並去克服障礙可能會

很具挑戰性，但只要擁有明確的目標意識、成長心態，以及樂於接受挑戰的意願，就能有助於個人去實現目標，進而創造出充實而有意義的人生。

The pursuit of purpose and meaning in life often requires sacrifice and hard work. There is a commonly held belief that in order to achieve something of value, one must be willing to pay the price. This can include sacrificing time, effort, or even personal desires in order to achieve a greater goal.

The idea that you have to pay the price you have to pay can be seen in many areas of life, from personal relationships to professional success. In order to achieve a healthy, fulfilling relationship, for example, individuals may need to make compromises and sacrifices for the benefit of both partners. In the workplace, individuals may need to put in long hours and make personal sacrifices in order to achieve professional success.

However, paying the price for one's goals is not always easy. It can require a great deal of determination, persistence, and resilience. It may also require a willingness to take risks and step outside of one's comfort zone.

One of the key factors in paying the price for one's goals is having a clear sense of purpose. When an individual has a strong sense of purpose, they are more likely to be willing to make sacrifices in order to achieve their goals. Purpose can provide the motivation and drive necessary to overcome obstacles and persevere through challenges.

Another important factor is mindset. Those who are able to pay the price for their goals often have a growth mindset, which is characterized by a belief in the ability to learn and grow through effort and experience. This mindset allows individuals to view challenges as opportunities for growth and to approach obstacles with resilience and determination.

It is also important to acknowledge that paying the price for one's goals is not always a linear process. There may be setbacks, failures, and unexpected challenges along the way. However, these challenges can be viewed as opportunities for growth and learning. By embracing these challenges and persisting through them, individuals can develop the skills and resilience necessary to achieve their goals.

In conclusion, the idea that you have to pay the price you have to pay is a fundamental concept in the pursuit of purpose and meaning in life. While it can be challenging to make sacrifices and overcome obstacles, having a clear sense of purpose, a growth mindset, and a willingness to embrace challenges can help individuals achieve their goals and create a fulfilling and meaningful life.

31

在金錢、時間和
熱情之間取得平衡

追尋人生目標，往往需要在金錢、時間和熱情三者之間找到一個巧妙的平衡。為了活得充實而有意義，我們就要妥善安排這些因素，並且用一種符合自己價值觀與目標意識的方式，來決定它們的優先順序。

金錢是實現許多目標的關鍵因素，因為它提供了追求熱情與充分利用時間所需要的資源。然而，重要的是要按照自己的價值觀和目標意識來決定金錢的優先順序。對某些人來說，財務安全可能最為重要，然而其他人可能會為了追求他們的熱情而把賺取一定程度的收入放在優先。終

究，重要的是要去反思金錢在我們的生命中究竟扮演什麼角色，並且要把我們的財務優先事項與我們的目標意識保持一致。

時間是找到人生目標和意義的另一個重要因素。我們選擇如何花費時間，會對我們的幸福與滿足感產生顯著的影響。重要的是要按照自己的價值觀和熱情來安排時間的優先順序。這可能意味著要抽出時間去參加能為我們帶來喜悅與滿足的活動，或是指要花時間去追求事業上或個人性質的目標。

在尋找人生目標上，熱情或許是最重要的因素。因為熱情就是一種能讓我們感到意義與滿足的東西，而且會為我們的生命帶來方向與目標。然而重要的是，在把熱情放在優先時，必須要以一種能夠符合我們財務與時間限制的方式來加以考量。這可能代表著要去找出方法來將熱情融入我們的專業或個人生活之中，也可能是指要去找到具創造性的方式來追求我們的熱情，就算還有其他必須要做的事情。

在安排財務、時間與熱情時，重要的是要去找到對我們個人來說是可行的平衡點。這也許意味著為了優先考慮

某個方面，就必須在另一方面做出犧牲。舉例來說，有可能是指為了追求工作之外的熱情，所以去做一份比較不讓人滿意的工作，或是為了達成財務上的安定，所以必須得要犧牲某些活動。

終究，適當安排財務、時間和熱情的關鍵，在於反思對我們個人來說什麼最重要。**透過把財務中的優先事項、時間及熱情，保持與價值觀和目標相一致，我們就能創造出更為充實和有意義的生活。**這可能需要做出艱難的選擇和犧牲，但最終的結果將會是一個更加與我們的真實自我與目標意識相符的人生。

The pursuit of purpose in life often requires a delicate balance between three key factors: money, time, and passion. In order to live a fulfilling and purposeful life, it is important to arrange these factors properly and prioritize them in a way that aligns with one's values and sense of purpose.

Money is a critical factor in achieving many of our goals, as it provides the resources necessary to pursue our passions and make the most of our time. However, it is important to prioritize money in a way that aligns with our values and sense of purpose. For some individuals, financial security may be the top priority, while others may prioritize earning a certain level of income in order to pursue their passions. Ultimately, it is important to reflect on what role money plays in our lives and to align our financial priorities with our sense of purpose.

Time is another critical factor in finding purpose and meaning in life. How we choose to spend our time can have a significant impact on our well-being and sense of fulfillment. It is important to prioritize our time in a way that aligns with our values and passions. This may mean setting aside time for activities that bring us joy and fulfillment, or it may mean dedicating time to pursuing professional or personal goals.

Passion is perhaps the most important factor in finding purpose in life. Our passions are the things that give us a sense of meaning and fulfillment, and they can provide direction and purpose in our lives. However, it is important to prioritize our passions in a way that aligns with our financial and time constraints. This may mean finding ways to incorporate our passions into our professional or personal lives, or it may mean finding creative ways to pursue our passions despite other obligations.

When arranging money, time, and passion, it is important to find a balance that works for us as individuals. This may mean making sacrifices in one area in order to prioritize another. For example, it may mean working a job that is less fulfilling in order to pursue a passion outside of work, or it may mean sacrificing certain activities in order to achieve financial stability.

Ultimately, the key to arranging money, time, and

passion properly is to reflect on what is most important to us as individuals. By aligning our financial priorities, time commitments, and passions with our values and sense of purpose, we can create a more fulfilling and meaningful life. This may require making difficult choices and sacrifices, but the end result can be a life that is more aligned with our true selves and our sense of purpose.

32

成功與否，
跟你堅持的力量成正比

尋找人生的目標與意義，往往需要許多努力與堅持。這可能會充滿挑戰性，因為要讓自己保有動力，並在面對挫折與障礙時還能專注於目標。然而，生命中的成功往往與持續的力量大小成正比，也就是說，那些能夠堅持克服挑戰並且不斷努力朝向目標邁進的人，終究比較能夠實現成功。

成功與持續力量大小成正比的觀點，其實根植於「堅持」的概念。堅持是一種去不斷克服挑戰與挫折的能力，並在面對逆境時還能保持決心與專注。那些在艱困時不屈

不撓的人比較能夠實現他們的目標，並在人生中找到目標與意義。

堅持的關鍵之一是要有明確的目標。**當個人有強烈的目標意識，他們就比較能夠在面對挑戰與挫折堅持到底。**因為目標可以提供克服障礙以及對長期目標保持專注所需要的動機與魄力。

堅持的另一個重要因素是具備成長心態。**成長心態的特點是相信藉由努力與經驗可以獲得學習與成長。這種心態能夠讓人把挑戰視為成長的機會，並且以韌性與決心來面對障礙。**

同時，重要的是要知道，堅持並不必然是不計代價地去完成挑戰。有時候，為了忠於個人的價值觀與目標意識，就是需要去重新評估目標並且調整方向。然而，即便是在這些情況下，堅持還是會在保持決心與專注上扮演一個重要的角色。

最後，要記住，堅持不是一種獨自完成的追求。來自他人的支持，例如朋友、家人及社群，都會扮演關鍵角色，讓我們能對長期目標保持動力並維持專注。因為尋求

他人的支持與鼓勵能有助於個人保持在正軌上，並在生活中維持目標意識與方向感。

　　總之，成功與持續力大小成正比的概念，點出了堅持的重要性。透過維持決心與專注、具有明確目標意識、培養成長心態，並且尋求他人支持，個人就能持續挑戰並達成他們的長期目標。儘管有時候堅持可能充滿挑戰性，但它終究會帶來更加充實而有意義的生命。

The pursuit of purpose and meaning in life often requires a great deal of effort and persistence. It can be challenging to stay motivated and focused on our goals in the face of setbacks and obstacles. However, success in life is often proportional to the magnitude of the force that continues, meaning that those who are able to persist through challenges and continue working towards their goals are more likely to achieve success in the long run.

The idea that success is proportional to the magnitude of the force that continues is rooted in the concept of perseverance. Perseverance is the ability to persist through challenges and setbacks, and to maintain a sense of determination and focus in the face of adversity. Those who are able to persevere through difficult times are more likely to achieve their goals and find purpose and meaning in their lives.

One of the keys to perseverance is having a clear sense of purpose. When an individual has a strong sense of purpose, they are more likely to be able to persist through challenges and setbacks. Purpose can provide the motivation and drive necessary to overcome obstacles and stay focused on long-term goals.

Another important factor in perseverance is having a growth mindset. A growth mindset is characterized by a belief in the ability to learn and grow through effort and experience. This mindset allows individuals to view challenges as opportunities for growth and to approach obstacles with resilience and determination.

It is also important to acknowledge that perseverance is not necessarily about pushing through challenges at all costs. There may be times when it is necessary to reassess goals and adjust course in order to stay true to one's values and sense of purpose. However, even in these situations, perseverance can play an important role in maintaining a sense of determination and focus.

Finally, it is important to remember that perseverance is not a solitary pursuit. The support of others, such as friends, family, and community, can play a critical role in maintaining motivation and staying focused on long-term goals. Seeking out support and encouragement from others can help individuals to stay on track and maintain a sense of purpose and direction in their lives.

In conclusion, the idea that success is proportional to the magnitude of the force that continues highlights the importance of perseverance. By maintaining a sense of determination and focus, having a clear sense of purpose, adopting a growth mindset, and seeking out support from others, individuals can persist through challenges and achieve their long-term goals. While perseverance may be challenging at times, it can ultimately lead to a more fulfilling and meaningful life.

33

誰都沒有可能現在就擁有一切

　　尋找人生目標與意義，往往需要做出困難的決定並且付出犧牲。它可能會充滿困難，因為要去權衡種種優先事項，並在所有生活面向中找出一種實現滿足的感覺。在某些狀況下，這可能代表著就是要去接受「不可能現在全都擁有」，並且去把生活中的某些面向，放在其他面向之前來優先考慮。

　　對於追求人生目標與意義來說，「我不可能現在就擁有一切」的想法是個重要概念。因為這是一項事實，就是**無論給予的時間有多長，我們所能達到的成就或經歷都是有限的**。然而，重要的是要知道，這並不代表要放棄我們

的目標或渴望。相反的，而是要更實際去面對什麼才是現在可能的，並去做出符合我們價值觀與目標意識的決定。

　　能夠優先考慮並做出困難決定的關鍵之一，就是具備明確的目標意識。當一個人具有強烈的目標意識，就比較能夠按照自己的價值觀來優先考慮目標並做出決定。意思是可能要去選擇專注於生活中的特定面向，例如職涯發展或是人際關係，以便就長遠來說能夠實現更大的滿足感。

　　另一個能夠做出艱難決定的重要因素，就是擁有成長心態。因為成長心態的特徵就是相信透過努力與經驗能夠獲得學習和成長。而這種心態能夠讓人把挫折與挑戰視為成長的機會，並用以一種決心與韌性的態度來處理困難的選擇。

　　同時，也要對此有所認知，就是做出困難抉擇並去優先考量生活中的某些面向，會是一個很不容易且令人不舒服的過程。它會需要放下特定願望或目標，或對生活中的某些方面做出犧牲以便能在另一些方面得到更大的成就感。然而，藉由實際面對什麼才是現在可能的事物，個人將能夠找到人生中更大的目標意識與意義。

此外，要記住，優先事項可能會隨著時間而改變。在生命中某個點上最重要的事物，也許在未來並不會那樣重要。透過對優先順序保持開放性並且順應環境的改變，個人就能隨著時間推移不斷在生活的不同領域中持續追求目標意識與成就感。

　　對於追求人生目標與意義來說，「我不可能現在就擁有一切」的想法很重要。**透過實際面對當下的可能性、擁有明確目標意識、具備成長型心態，並以開放性來適應時間變化，個人將能做出艱難選擇，進而在生命中找到更大的成就感和意義。**

The pursuit of purpose in life often requires making difficult choices and sacrifices. It can be challenging to balance competing priorities and find a sense of fulfillment in all aspects of life. In some cases, this may mean acknowledging that it is not possible to have it all right now, and prioritizing certain areas of life over others.

The idea that "I can't have it all right now" is an important concept in the pursuit of purpose and meaning in life. It is a recognition that there are limitations to what we can achieve or experience at any given time. However, it is important to acknowledge that this does not mean giving up on our goals or aspirations. Rather, it means being realistic about what is possible in the present moment, and making choices that are aligned with our values and sense of purpose.

One key aspect of prioritizing and making difficult choices is having a clear sense of purpose. When an individual has a strong sense of purpose, they are better able to prioritize their goals and make choices that align with their values. This may mean choosing to focus on a particular aspect of life, such as career or personal relationships, in order to achieve greater fulfillment in the long run.

Another important factor in making difficult choices is having a growth mindset. A growth mindset is characterized by a belief in the ability to learn and grow through effort and experience. This mindset allows individuals to view setbacks and challenges as opportunities for growth, and to approach difficult choices with a sense of determination and resilience.

It is also important to acknowledge that making difficult choices and prioritizing certain areas of life can be a difficult and uncomfortable process. It may require letting go of certain aspirations or goals, or making sacrifices in one area of life in order to achieve greater fulfillment in another. However, by being realistic about what is possible in the present moment, individuals can find a greater sense of purpose and meaning in their lives.

In addition, it is important to remember that priorities can shift over time. What may be a top priority at one point in life may not be as important in the future. By being open to shifting priorities and adapting to changing circumstances, individuals can continue to pursue their sense of purpose and find fulfillment in different areas of life over time.

The idea that "I can't have it all right now" is an important concept in the pursuit of purpose and meaning in life. By being realistic about what is possible in the present moment, having a clear sense of purpose, adopting a growth mindset, and being open to shifting priorities over time, individuals can make difficult choices and find a greater sense of fulfillment and meaning in their lives.

34

做事情的方式，
和所做出來的事情同樣重要

對於人生目標與意義的追求，並不僅僅在於達成某些
目標或成就，而是關乎我們如何在這個世界上為人處事。
在許多情況下，我們怎麼去做，就跟我們做出什麼一樣重
要，因為我們的行為與態度會對自己及周遭他人的福祉都
產生重大影響。

品格是影響我們言行舉止的一大關鍵。而我們的品格
則是素養與特質的組合，它定義了我們是誰以及我們如何
與這個世界互動。這可能包括誠實、正直、同理心以及同
情心等人格特點。透過培養堅強的品格，我們就能與他人

建構出一種正向的關係，進而對世界做出有意義的貢獻。

態度則是影響我們行為的另一個重要面向。**我們的態度會嚴重影響到我們如何體驗世界，以及別人如何看待我們。**一種積極的態度，具有樂觀、韌性以及願意學習的特點，能幫助我們克服挑戰並達成目標。相反的，消極的態度，像是憤世嫉俗、悲觀及缺乏動力等特徵，則會束縛我們，讓我們沒有辦法活得充實而有目標。

我們如何為人處事也跟我們的價值觀與信仰緊密相關。因為價值觀與信仰塑造出我們看待這個世界以及我們與他人互動的方式。所以**透過讓言行舉止與價值觀及信仰保持一致，我們才能活得比較真切充實，並且能對周遭他人的福祉有所貢獻。**

同時，也要明白，我們的言行舉止不僅關乎個人的行為，也跟我們如何與他人互動有關。我們的所作所為會對身邊的人產生顯著的影響，無論是透過言語、行為或是態度。透過與他人培養正面的關係並以尊重及同理心來對待他們，我們將能夠對這個世界做出有意義的貢獻。

總之，「我們怎麼去做，就跟我們做出什麼一樣重

要」的觀念，對於追求人生目標與意義來說非常重要。透過培養堅強的品格、保持積極的態度、讓行為舉止符合我們的價值觀和信仰，並且以尊重和同理心來對待他人，我們才能活得更加充實、更有意義，並對周遭的世界產生正面的影響。

The pursuit of purpose and meaning in life is not just about achieving certain goals or accomplishments; it is also about how we behave and conduct ourselves in the world. In many cases, how we behave is just as important as what we do, as our actions and attitudes can have a significant impact on our well-being and the well-being of those around us.

One key aspect of how we behave is our character. Our character is the set of qualities and attributes that define who we are and how we interact with the world. This may include traits such as honesty, integrity, compassion, and empathy. By cultivating a strong character, we can build positive relationships with others and make a meaningful contribution to the world.

Another important aspect of how we behave is our attitude. Our attitude can have a significant impact on how we experience the world, as well as how we are perceived by others. A positive attitude, characterized by optimism, resilience, and a willingness to learn, can help us to overcome challenges and achieve our goals. Conversely, a negative attitude, characterized by cynicism, pessimism, and a lack of motivation, can hold us back and prevent us from living a fulfilling and purposeful life.

How we behave is also closely tied to our values and beliefs. Our values and beliefs shape how we see the world and how we interact with others. By aligning our behavior with our values and beliefs, we can live a more authentic and fulfilling life, while also contributing to the well-being of those around us.

It is also important to acknowledge that how we behave is not just about our individual actions, but also about how we interact with others. Our behavior can have a significant impact on the well-being of those around us, whether it is through our words, actions, or attitudes. By cultivating positive relationships with others and treating them with respect and compassion, we can make a meaningful contribution to the world.

In conclusion, the idea that how we behave is as important as what we do is a critical concept in the pursuit of purpose and meaning in life. By cultivating a strong character, maintaining a positive attitude, aligning our behavior with our values and beliefs, and treating others with respect and compassion, we can live a more fulfilling and purposeful life, while also making a positive impact on the world around us.

35

重視過程，而不只是結果

　　追求人生的目標和意義，往往涉及設定方向與努力達標。然而，重要的是要記住，致力朝向這些目標的過程，就和最後的結果一樣重要。因為在許多狀況下，我們為了實現目標而採行的方式，以及為了向目標邁進而展開的旅程，就跟最終成果一樣令人感到充實而具有意義。

　　重視過程而非結果的一大關鍵，就是抱持成長心態。成長心態的特點在於相信透過努力與經驗可以獲得學習與成長。所以**當我們以一種成長心態來接近目標，就比較能專注在致力邁向目標過程中得到的學習與成長，而不只是聚焦在最後結果。**

重視過程而非結果的另一重要面向，則是培養覺察意識。覺察就是全然專注於當下，不帶任何判斷或分心。藉由帶著覺察意識去接近我們的目標，我們將更能完全的欣賞這趟為了達標而展開的旅程，並且在過程中找到更大的滿足感與意義。

同時也要認知，致力朝向我們目標的過程也許不可預測並且充滿不確定性。沿途中可能會遭遇挫折、挑戰還有障礙。然而，就是透過這些經驗，我們才有學習與成長的機會，並且在我們的生命中找到更大的目標與意義。

此外，要重視過程而不只是結果，還必須從構成我們日常生活的渺小時刻與經驗之中找到喜悅與滿足。而透過培養一種對於當下的感謝與珍惜的心態，就能從生命中找到更大的喜悅與滿足感，無論我們的目標最後結果如何。

總之，「過程與結果一樣重要」的想法，對於追求人生目標與意義來說很重要。藉由抱持成長心態、培養覺察意識、接受邁向目標旅程中的不確定性及挑戰性，並且在日常生活的微小時刻中尋求喜悅與滿足，我們才能活得更加充實而有意義。**<u>儘管實現目標也很重要，但最後定義我們的目標意識與滿足感的，卻正是朝向那些目標的旅程。</u>**

The pursuit of purpose and meaning in life often involves setting and working towards goals. However, it is important to remember that the process of working towards these goals is just as important as the ultimate result. In many cases, the way in which we approach our goals and the journey we take towards achieving them can be just as fulfilling and meaningful as the end result.

One key aspect of valuing the process over the result is adopting a growth mindset. A growth mindset is characterized by a belief in the ability to learn and grow through effort and experience. When we approach our goals with a growth mindset, we are more likely to focus on the learning and growth that comes from the process of working towards our goals, rather than just on the end result.

Another important aspect of valuing the process over the result is cultivating a sense of mindfulness. Mindfulness involves being fully present in the moment, without judgment or distraction. By approaching our goals with a sense of mindfulness, we can more fully appreciate the journey we are taking towards achieving our goals, and find greater fulfillment and meaning in the process.

It is also important to acknowledge that the process of working towards our goals can be unpredictable and uncertain. We may encounter setbacks, challenges, and obstacles along the way. However, it is through these experiences that we have the opportunity to learn and grow, and to find a greater sense of purpose and meaning in our lives.

In addition, valuing the process over the result can also involve finding joy and fulfillment in the small moments and experiences that make up our daily lives. By cultivating a sense of gratitude and appreciation for the present moment, we can find greater joy and fulfillment in our lives, regardless of the ultimate outcome of our goals.

In conclusion, the idea that the process is as important as the result is a critical concept in the pursuit of purpose and meaning in life. By adopting a growth mindset, cultivating a sense of mindfulness, embracing the uncertainty and challenges of the journey towards our goals, and finding joy and fulfillment in the small moments of our daily lives, we can live a more fulfilling and meaningful life. While achieving our goals may be important, it is the journey towards those goals that ultimately defines our sense of purpose and fulfillment.

Chpater 6.
讓情緒成為成功的助力

此圖為AI以書名、目錄和主題為指令而繪製的封面初稿之一。

在追求成功的過程中，我們往往會試圖壓抑或忽視我們的情緒。然而，情緒可能會是有助於我們實現目標的強大工具。在第六章中，我們就來探討如何以一種能夠幫助我們成功的方式來運用情緒。

首先，我們需要理解「面對面」這個詞的真正含義。這代表著要去正視我們的情緒、承認它們，然後採取行動。請不要去否認我們的感受，而是要去學習如何運用它們來當作我們行動的指南。

其次，則是在自然中學習生命的法則。大自然是出色的老師，能夠教我們如何取得情感與理智的平衡。就像太陽和雨一起創造生命，我們也可以學習如何將情感與邏輯合起來運用以達成我們的目標。

我們也應該注意我們所使用的言語，無論是對自己還

是對其他人。因為藉由重複使用積極的肯定語句及授予權力的語言，我們就能以一種有助於實現成功的方式來影響我們的思想和情緒。

冥想可以成為幫助我們管理情緒的有用工具。透過定期練習，我們可以學習不帶任何判斷地觀察自己的思想和感受，讓我們能用一種更具成效的方式來回應它們。

儘管情緒能有所幫助，但我們也必須學習客觀看待問題，只使用邏輯事實而不受感情左右。因為這種方法能幫助我們做出更理性的決策，進而獲得更成功的結果。

很重要的是要有所認知，每個人都有偏見，包括我們自己。透過承認我們的偏見並努力克服它們，我們可以做出更好的決策，並建立更堅固的人際關係。

有時候，即使我們是對的，還是會有人不聽我們的話。在這種情況下，我們可以專注於當下，無論在身體上還是情感上。因為全然投入當下能幫助我們更有效地溝通，並且與他人建立更強的連結。

存在不僅僅是一種表現，也是一種生活方式。透過體

現存在，我們可以培養必要的情商，讓我們在個人與職業生活中獲得成功。

此外，最能看出一個人真正品格的方法之一，就是賦予他們權力。透過觀察某人在掌權之後的行為舉止，我們就更能理解他們的價值觀和動機。

最後，我們還需要對於自己何時情緒失控能有所警覺。因為儘管情緒能對我們有所助益，但它也會混淆我們的判斷、導致糟糕的決策。而透過認知到情緒何時控制我們，我們就能往後退一步，並且更加客觀地處理情況。

情緒是我們生命中不可缺少的一個部分。透過學習如何用一種有助於成功的方式來使用它們，能幫助我們實現目標、讓我們活得更加充實。但這並不是要去壓抑我們的情緒，而是要學習去取得情緒、邏輯與理性之間的平衡，好讓我們能夠做出更好的決策，進而建立出更加強大的人際關係。

In our pursuit of success, we often try to suppress or ignore our emotions. However, emotions can be powerful tools that help us achieve our goals. In Chapter 6, we will explore how to use emotions in a way that helps us succeed.

Firstly, we need to understand the true meaning of the word "face-to-face." This means facing our emotions, acknowledging them, and then taking action. It's not about denying our feelings but rather learning to use them as a compass for our actions.

Next, we can learn the logic of life in nature. Nature is an excellent teacher of how to balance our emotions with reason. Just as the sun and the rain work together to create life, we can learn to use our emotions and logic together to achieve our goals.

We should also pay attention to the words we use, both to ourselves and to others. By repeating positive affirmations and using empowering language, we can influence our thoughts and emotions in a way that helps us achieve success.

Meditation can be a useful tool in helping us manage our emotions. Through regular practice, we can learn to observe our thoughts and feelings without judgment, allowing us to respond to them in a more productive way.

While emotions can be helpful, we must also learn to look at problems objectively, using only logical facts without being swayed by our feelings. This approach allows us to make more rational decisions, leading to more successful outcomes.

It's important to recognize that everyone is prejudiced, including ourselves. By acknowledging our biases and working to overcome them, we can make better decisions and build stronger relationships.

Sometimes, there will be people who don't listen, no matter how right we may be. In these situations, we can focus on being present, both physically and emotionally. Being fully engaged in the moment can help us communicate more effectively and build stronger connections with others.

Presence is not just an act; it's a way of being. By embodying presence, we can cultivate the emotional intelligence necessary to succeed in our personal and professional lives.

One of the surest ways to recognize a person's true character is to give them authority. By observing how someone behaves when given power, we can better understand their values and motivations.

Finally, we need to be aware of when our emotions get out of control. While they can be helpful, they can also cloud our judgment and lead to poor decision-making. By recognizing when our emotions are taking over, we can take a step back and approach the situation more objectively.

Emotions are an essential part of our lives. By learning to use them in a way that helps us succeed, we can achieve our goals and live more fulfilling lives. It's not about suppressing our emotions, but rather learning to balance them with logic and reason, allowing us to make better decisions and build stronger relationships.

36

必須先正視現實，
才有辦法改變

面對現實是找到人生目標的重要步驟。正視事實可能很困難，但只有承認和接受現實，我們才能向前邁進並做出積極的改變。在這一章中，我們將探討面對現實的真正含義，以及它能如何幫助我們找到人生目標。

面對現實，意味著要去承認我們的處境真相，無論它有多麼困難或痛苦。它需要我們去對自己和他人誠實，即使這會令人很不舒服。透過面對現實，我們可以確認需要做出改變的地方，並且採取行動去為自己創造一個更美好的未來。

<u>面對現實的最大的挑戰之一，就是處理自己的情緒。</u>
去否認或避開難以對付的情緒，可能很容易，但這只會延
長問題。所以我們反而必須學會以健康的方式去承認並處
理我們的情緒，這樣才能帶著清晰的思維與堅定的目標意
識向前邁進。

　　面對現實的另一個重要面向，則是願意為自己的生命
負責。<u>我們無法改變過去，但可以採取行動去創造美好的
未來。</u>透過對自己的行動和選擇負責，我們不但能重新獲
得對生命的掌控感，並且還能開始向積極的方向邁進。

　　儘管面對現實可能是一個困難和痛苦的過程，但對於
找到人生目標和意義來說，它終究是必要的。正如同美國
作家和詩人瑪雅‧安吉洛所說：「我會被發生在我身上的
事所改變，但我拒絕被它消耗」。透過面對現實，我們就
能克服挑戰，並且變得比從前更加強大、更有韌性。

Facing reality is an essential step in finding purpose in life. It can be difficult to confront the truth, but it is only by acknowledging and accepting reality that we can move forward and make positive changes. In this chapter, we will explore the true meaning of facing reality and how it can help us find purpose in life.

Facing reality means acknowledging the truth of our situation, no matter how difficult or painful it may be. It requires us to be honest with ourselves and others, even when it is uncomfortable. By facing reality, we can identify the areas where we need to make changes and take steps towards creating a better future for ourselves.

One of the biggest challenges of facing reality is dealing with our own emotions. It can be easy to deny or avoid difficult emotions, but this only prolongs the problem. Instead, we must learn to acknowledge and process our emotions in a healthy way, so that we can move forward with a clear mind and a strong sense of purpose.

Another important aspect of facing reality is being willing

to take responsibility for our own lives. We cannot change the past, but we can take steps towards creating a better future. By taking responsibility for our own actions and choices, we can regain a sense of control over our lives and start moving in a positive direction.

Facing reality can be a difficult and painful process, but it is ultimately necessary for finding purpose and meaning in our lives. As American author and poet Maya Angelou once said, "I can be changed by what happens to me. But I refuse to be reduced by it." By facing reality, we can overcome our challenges and emerge stronger and more resilient than before.

37

向大自然學習生命的法則

在自然中學習生命的法則，可以提供我們寶貴的見解，幫助我們找到人生目標與意義。大自然有一種和諧、平衡且相互關聯的運作方式。透過學習和觀察自然界，我們可以更容易了解怎麼去用一種平衡與和諧的方式來與自己及周遭世界共存。

我們能從大自然學到的最重要一課，就是萬物相互關聯。正如美國環保主義者及作家約翰・緬爾所說：「當我們試圖將任何事物獨立出來，就會發現它和宇宙中的其他一切都緊密相連。」換句話說，每件事物都彼此連結、互相依存，我們必須共同努力來維持自然界的這個平衡。

我們能從自然界學到的另外一課，則是適應性與韌性的重要性。自然界不斷變化，生物必須適應才能生存。同樣的，當生活中面臨挑戰與改變時，我們也必須學會適應而有彈性。

　　自然也可以教導我們關於休息和恢復的重要性。正如同冬季時動物會冬眠、植物會進入休眠，我們也需要休息和恢復的時間來補充能量、恢復活力。

　　最後，大自然還能啟發我們在生活中找到目標與意義。無論透過花時間去享受自然，或是致力於保護環境，藉由與大自然連結，我們都能找到一種目標意識與滿足的感受。

　　總之，從自然中學習生命的法則可以成為我們尋找人生目標與意義的有力工具。**透過學習和觀察自然界，我們能更加理解如何去用一種平衡和諧的方法來與我們自己及周遭世界共存。**正如美國作家和博物學家亨利・大衛・梭羅所說：「隨著每個季節的來去生活，呼吸空氣，暢飲酒水，品味果實，就讓自己順應大地的牽動」。

Learning the logic of life in nature can provide us with valuable insights that can help us find purpose and meaning in our own lives. Nature has a way of operating that is harmonious, balanced, and interconnected. By studying and observing the natural world, we can gain a better understanding of how to live in balance and harmony with ourselves and the world around us.

One of the most important lessons we can learn from nature is the interconnectedness of all things. As American environmentalist and writer John Muir once said, "When we try to pick out anything by itself, we find it hitched to everything else in the Universe." In other words, everything is connected and interdependent, and we must work together to maintain the balance of the natural world.

Another lesson we can learn from nature is the importance of adaptation and resilience. The natural world is constantly changing, and organisms must adapt to survive. In the same way, we must learn to be adaptable and resilient in the face of challenges and changes in our own lives.

Nature can also teach us about the importance of rest and rejuvenation. Just as animals hibernate or plants go dormant in the winter, we too need periods of rest and rejuvenation to replenish our energy and restore our vitality.

Finally, nature can inspire us to find purpose and meaning in our own lives. Whether it's by spending time in nature or working to protect the environment, we can find a sense of purpose and fulfillment by connecting with the natural world.

In conclusion, learning the logic of life in nature can be a powerful tool for finding purpose and meaning in our own lives. By studying and observing the natural world, we can gain a better understanding of how to live in balance and harmony with ourselves and the world around us. As American writer and naturalist Henry David Thoreau once said, "Live in each season as it passes; breathe the air, drink the drink, taste the fruit, and resign yourself to the influence of the earth. "

38

從對方的立場思考對話，
才能真正有效溝通

有效溝通是找到人生目標的一大關鍵。而溝通最重要的要素之一，就是要能從另一個人的觀點來看待事物。所以透過**重複某人使用過的詞彙和語句，可以讓我們更加理解對方的觀點，並且建立更緊密的連結**。在這一章中，我們將探索從另一個人的角度重複言詞語句的重要性，以及這樣做能如何幫助我們找到人生目標。

重複別人的措辭用語，代表我們正在積極聆聽並努力理解對方的觀點。這有助於建立信任感，並創造更有意義的對話。透過把自己放在他人的立場，我們就能更加理解

他們的想法、感受以及動機。而這有助於培養同理心與理解力，並且帶來更堅固的人際關係、更強大的目標意識。

當我們重複別人的言詞語句時，需要注意自己的語調和肢體語言。我們應該用開放的心態和願意學習的態度來進行對話。透過積極聆聽他人的話語，我們才能找到新的方法去解決問題並建立更深厚的關係。

總之，重複別人所用過的言詞話語，可以成為有效溝通的強大工具。它能幫助我們建立信任、獲得同理心、跨越鴻溝、找到共同點。而**透過有意義的對話並積極傾聽他人，我們就能在生活中找到更深遠的目標和意義**。美國作家和哲學家拉爾夫・沃爾多・愛默生曾說：「擁有朋友的唯一方法，就是成為一個朋友。」而這句話也提醒我們，真正的溝通和連結，建立在相互理解與同理心的基礎上。

Effective communication is a crucial aspect of finding purpose in life. One of the most important components of communication is being able to see things from another person's perspective. By repeating the words and phrases that someone else uses, we can better understand their point of view and build stronger connections. In this chapter, we will explore the importance of repeating words and phrases from another person's point of view and how it can help us find purpose in life.

Repeating someone else's words and phrases shows that we are actively listening and trying to understand their perspective. It can help build trust and create a more meaningful conversation. By putting ourselves in someone else's shoes, we can gain a better understanding of their thoughts, feelings, and motivations. This can help us develop empathy and understanding, leading to stronger relationships and a greater sense of purpose.

When we repeat someone else's words and phrases, we need to be mindful of our tone and body language. We should approach the conversation with an open mind and a willingness to learn. By actively listening to others, we can find new ways to approach problems and build stronger relationships.

In conclusion, repeating the words and phrases that someone else uses can be a powerful tool for effective communication. It can help us build trust, gain empathy, bridge divides, and find common ground. By engaging in meaningful conversations and actively listening to others, we can find greater purpose and meaning in our lives. As American writer and philosopher Ralph Waldo Emerson once said, "The only way to have a friend is to be one." This quote reminds us that true communication and connection are built on mutual understanding and empathy.

39

透過冥想看見內在，
找到更深層的目標與意義

冥想是尋找人生目標和意義的強大工具。透過練習覺察，並把注意力聚焦於當下，我們才能更加了解自己以及周圍的世界。在本章中，我們就要來探討冥想能帶給我們的好處，以及它將如何幫助我們找到人生目標。

冥想最重要的好處之一，就是增加自我意識。透過把注意力放在我們的想法、情緒以及身體的感受，我們就能對自己和內心運作有更深的了解。這可以幫助我們去辨別可能會對我們造成阻礙的模式和行為，並對我們的生活造成積極的改變。

冥想也能有助於我們去開發對於他人的更大同理心與理解力。藉由培養同情心以及不帶判斷的意識，我們才能學會從不同角度去看待世界，並且與他人建立起更深厚的關係。

冥想的另一個好處則是增強注意力與專心。藉由訓練大腦去專注於當下，我們可以發展出更清晰的思維和更高的效率。這能幫助我們實現目標，進而在生活中找到更大的成就感。

冥想也可以成為管理壓力和焦慮的有力工具。透過練習覺察與深呼吸，我們能夠學會放鬆身心，擺脫負面思考和情緒。這能有助於我們找到更大的內在平靜與平衡，即便置身於艱困的環境。

最後，冥想可以幫助我們與自己的靈性自我連接，並且找到更大的人生意義與目標。因為透過培養感謝心並與天地連接，我們就能進入更深層的目標與滿足意識。

總之，對於尋找人生目標與意義來說，冥想是一項寶貴的工具。**透過練習覺察並且把我們的注意力聚焦在當下，我們就能獲得更多的自我意識、同理心、專注力和**

內在平靜。正如美國作家和哲學家拉爾夫・沃爾多・愛默生所說：「比起我們內在的事物，我們身後和眼前的事物，都微不足道」。藉由冥想的練習，我們將能進入內在的自己，並且在生命中找到更大的目的和意義。

Meditation is a powerful tool for finding purpose and meaning in life. By practicing mindfulness and focusing our attention on the present moment, we can gain a better understanding of ourselves and the world around us. In this chapter, we will explore some of the things that we can get from meditation and how it can help us find purpose in life.

One of the most important benefits of meditation is increased self-awareness. By focusing our attention on our thoughts, feelings, and bodily sensations, we can gain a better understanding of ourselves and our own inner workings. This can help us identify patterns and behaviors that may be holding us back and make positive changes in our lives.

Meditation can also help us develop greater empathy

and understanding towards others. By cultivating a sense of compassion and non-judgmental awareness, we can learn to see the world from different perspectives and build stronger relationships with others.

Another benefit of meditation is increased focus and concentration. By training our minds to focus on the present moment, we can develop greater mental clarity and productivity. This can help us achieve our goals and find greater fulfillment in our lives.

Meditation can also be a powerful tool for managing stress and anxiety. By practicing mindfulness and deep breathing, we can learn to relax and let go of negative thoughts and emotions. This can help us find greater inner peace and balance, even in the midst of challenging circumstances.

Finally, meditation can help us connect with our spiritual selves and find greater meaning and purpose in life. By cultivating a sense of gratitude and connection with the universe, we can tap into a deeper sense of purpose and fulfillment.

In conclusion, meditation is a valuable tool for finding purpose and meaning in life. By practicing mindfulness and focusing our attention on the present moment, we can gain greater self-awareness, empathy, focus, and inner peace. As American writer and philosopher Ralph Waldo Emerson once said, "What lies behind us and what lies before us are tiny matters compared to what lies within us." Through the practice of meditation, we can tap into our inner selves and find greater purpose and meaning in our lives.

40

只用邏輯事實來看待問題，不受情感操控

不受情感左右、單純以邏輯事實來看待問題的能力，是尋找人生目標與意義的重要技能。因為情緒往往會干擾判斷、讓我們偏離方向，導致難以做出清晰而理性的決定。所以在這一章中，我們將探討只用邏輯事實來看待問題的力量，以及它將如何幫助我們找到人生的目標。

只從邏輯事實來看待問題的最大好處之一，就是能夠做出清晰而合理的決策。**透過去把複雜情況中的情感因素刪除，我們就能更加客觀的分析情況，並且依據最有效果、最有效率的方式來做出決定。**這會有助於我們實現目

標，並在生活中獲得更大的成就感。

能優雅、鎮定面對困境的能力，則是憑邏輯事實看待問題的另一個好處。透過避免衝動反應並採取更謹慎的作法，我們就能保持冷靜，做出符合自己最大利益的決定。

需要注意的是，情感是人類經驗中不可或缺的一部分，不應該被完全忽視。但是，在解決問題和做出決定時，保持情緒冷靜並仰賴邏輯和理性，還是非常重要。

只用邏輯事實來看待問題並不容易，因為要把情感從複雜的情況中刪除，可能會很具挑戰性。然而，透過練習，我們可以培養出客觀分析情勢所需要的技能，並且依據最有效果與效率的原則來做出決定。

也正因為這樣，只用邏輯事實來看待問題的能力，對於尋找人生目標與意義來說，是一項很重要的工具。藉由從複雜情勢中去除情感的影響，我們才能清晰而理性的做出符合我們最大利益的決策。正如希臘哲學家亞里士多德所說：「**能夠懷抱一種思想而不一定全盤接受它，就是一個人受過教育的標誌。**」透過學會帶著批判性與客觀性去思考，才能發展出尋找人生目標與滿足感所需要的技能。

The power to look at problems with only logical facts, without being clouded by emotions, is a critical skill for finding purpose and meaning in life. Emotions can often cloud our judgment and lead us astray, making it difficult to make clear and rational decisions. In this chapter, we will explore the power of looking at problems with only logical facts and how it can help us find purpose in life.

One of the most important benefits of looking at problems with only logical facts is the ability to make clear and rational decisions. By removing emotions from the equation, we can analyze the situation objectively and make decisions based on what is most effective and efficient. This can help us achieve our goals and find greater fulfillment in our lives.

Another benefit of looking at problems with only logical facts is the ability to handle difficult situations with grace and composure. By avoiding knee-jerk reactions and taking a more measured approach, we can maintain our composure and make decisions that are in our best interest.

It's important to note that emotions are an essential

part of the human experience and should not be dismissed entirely. However, when it comes to solving problems and making decisions, it's important to keep emotions in check and rely on logic and reason.

Looking at problems with only logical facts is not always easy, as it can be challenging to remove emotions from the equation. However, with practice, we can develop the skills needed to analyze situations objectively and make decisions based on what is most effective and efficient.

For that reason, the power of looking at problems with only logical facts is a critical skill for finding purpose and meaning in life. By removing emotions from the equation, we can make clear and rational decisions that are in our best interest. As Greek philosopher Aristotle once said, "It is the mark of an educated mind to be able to entertain a thought without accepting it." By learning to think critically and objectively, we can develop the skills needed to find purpose and fulfillment in our lives.

41

偏見存在於我們每個人之中

在我們這個世界上，偏見是一個不幸的現實，而且它可能會成為尋找人生目標與意義的主要障礙。重要的是要知道，每個人都有偏見和成見，無論自己是否意識到它們的存在。在這一章，我們將探討偏見這個主題，以及它會如何影響我們尋找目標和實現自我的能力。

解決偏見的第一步，是要知道它的存在。基於我們的成長過程、經驗和文化背景不同，所有人都有自己的偏見和成見。而透過承認並解決這些偏見，我們將可以開始打破我們與他人的隔閡。

擺脫偏見的另一個重點，則是要去學習對他人更具同理心與理解力。藉由尋求理解那些與我們不同的觀點和經驗，我們才能開始去跨越存在於社會之中的鴻溝。

　　還有一件事很重要，就是要注意偏見會影響我們生活的方式。因為偏見會讓我們對他人預設立場，而這將限制我們去建構有意義的連結以及尋找人生目標的能力。

　　最後，當看到偏見與歧視時，我們要能夠願意說出來對抗。透過支持正義並擁護他人的權利，我們才能去幫助開創一個更加公正與平等的社會。

　　偏見是尋找人生目標與意義的重大障礙。**透過承認自身的偏見，並且努力對他人更有同理心與理解力，我們就能打破隔閡，進而建立更強大的連結。**正如美國民權運動人士與作家奧德瑞‧洛德所說：「分裂我們的不是我們的不同，而是我們無法認識、接受和慶祝這些不同。」透過頌揚我們的不同並致力解決偏見，我們將能在生命中找到更大的目標和意義。

Prejudice is an unfortunate reality in our world, and it can be a major obstacle to finding purpose and meaning in life. It's important to recognize that everyone has their own biases and prejudices, whether they are conscious of them or not. In this chapter, we will explore the topic of prejudice and how it can impact our ability to find purpose and fulfillment.

The first step in addressing prejudice is to recognize that it exists. We all have our own biases and prejudices based on our upbringing, experiences, and cultural background. By acknowledging and addressing these biases, we can start to break down the barriers that separate us from others.

Another important aspect of addressing prejudice is learning to be more empathetic and understanding towards others. By seeking to understand the perspectives and experiences of those who are different from us, we can begin to bridge the divides that exist in our society.

It's also important to be aware of the ways that prejudice can impact our own lives. Prejudice can lead us to make assumptions about others, which can limit our ability to form meaningful connections and find purpose in our lives.

Finally, we need to be willing to speak out against prejudice and discrimination when we see it. By standing up for what is right and advocating for the rights of others, we can help create a more just and equitable society.

Prejudice is a significant barrier to finding purpose and meaning in life. By acknowledging our own biases and working to be more empathetic and understanding towards others, we can break down the barriers that separate us and build stronger connections. As American civil rights activist and writer Audre Lorde once said, "It is not our differences that divide us. It is our inability to recognize, accept, and celebrate those differences." By celebrating our differences and working to address prejudice, we can find greater purpose and meaning in our lives.

42

即便你說的話再對，
也別強迫另一個人接受

我們常常會遇到有人就是不聽勸告，不管你有多努力試圖去說服他們。而這種情況會讓人感到很沮喪，特別是當你真心想要幫助他們找到人生目標時。

然而，重要的是要記住，**每個人都有自己獨特的旅程，對一個人有效的方法，未必對另一個人有效。**所以儘管你說的話可能是對的，但如果某個人還沒有準備好或不願意聽，那麼你的努力也可能會落空。

有句名諺完美詮釋了這個觀念，就是：「你可以把馬

帶到水邊，但你無法強迫牠喝水。」這個金句已經流傳好幾世紀，並且就是在提醒我們不要強迫別人去做他們還沒準備好的事情，即便我們知道那對他們有好處。

與其試圖強加我們的想法或建議給他人，我們可以專注於成為他們生命中的支持者。我們可以傾聽他們，在他們要求時提供指引，並在他們的旅程中給予鼓勵。雖然最終每個人都只能靠自己去找到人生目標，但我們可以成為他們生命旅程中有所助益的伴侶。

It's common to encounter people who don't seem to listen to good advice, no matter how much you try to convince them. This can be frustrating, especially if you're genuinely trying to help them find their purpose in life.

However, it's essential to remember that everyone has their own unique journey, and what works for one person may not work for another. You may be saying the right things, but if someone isn't ready or willing to hear them, your efforts may fall on deaf ears.

One famous saying that encapsulates this idea is, "You can lead a horse to water, but you can't make it drink." This proverb has been around for centuries and reminds us that we can't force someone to do something they're not ready for, even if we know it's good for them.

Instead of trying to force our ideas or advice on others, we can focus on being a supportive presence in their lives. We can listen to them, offer guidance when they ask for it, and provide encouragement along the way. Ultimately, it's up to each person to find their own purpose in life, but we can be a helpful companion on their journey.

43

存在感來自於做對的事，
而不是做很多事

在步調很快的現今社會中，我們往往發現自己奔跑在一個任務與行動永無止境的機器上。我們試圖在追求幸福和成就的過程中完成更多、獲得更多，並做得更多。但到頭來，我們常常只感到不知所措、壓力重重、無法滿足，儘管我們那麼努力。而這是因為我們所追求的是錯的事物，並與我們的內在目標與存在感失散。

存在感是一種完全在當下的狀態。它是找到人生目標、活得充實的關鍵。當我們存在於當下，會對周遭的種種可能性和機會保持開放性，並且能夠運用內在智慧與直

覺來引導我們走向真正的目標。

存在感不是要去做得更多，而是要去投入得更深。它關乎對我們所做的每一件事去培養出一種覺醒、專注與用心的深刻意識。當我們存在，不會被過去或未來所分心，而是完全投入於當下，我們的行動也會變得更加有目的、有計劃，也更有效果。

正確的行動是符合我們內在目標與價值觀的作為。它不是要我們去做很多事情，而是要我們去做真正重要的事情。當我們存在於當下，就能從種種活動中分辨出正確的行動，並將我們的能量和資源集中在真正重要的事物上。

以下是培養存在意識進而正確行動的一些方法：

1.練習覺察：覺察是全神貫注參與當下的練習。它是培養存在意識、減少壓力並增進整體幸福感的強大工具。

2.與自然連結：與大自然共處能幫助我們跟自己的內在目標連結，並且為我們的思緒帶來平靜和清晰的感覺。

3.反思你的價值觀和目標：花時間去想想你的核心價

值觀與長期目標。這將有助於你將自己的行動以及內在目標與價值觀保持一致。

4.簡化生活：把生活簡單化可以幫助你減少干擾、清理思緒，並為當下和目標創造出更多空間。

5.擁抱寂靜：在你的一天中去擁有一些安靜的時刻，無論是通過冥想、祈禱，或者就只是靜下來。這可以幫助自己跟內在智慧與直覺產生連結。

總之，要有存在意識進而採取正確行動，而不是去做很多事情。藉由培養存在感，我們才能更加靠近內在目標，使行動與價值觀一致，並且活得更加充實而有意義。

In today's fast-paced world, we often find ourselves running on a treadmill of never-ending tasks and activities. We try to accomplish more, acquire more, and do more in our pursuit of happiness and fulfillment. But often, we end up feeling overwhelmed, stressed, and unfulfilled, despite our efforts. It is because we are chasing the wrong things and have lost touch with our inner purpose and presence.

Presence is the state of being fully present and engaged in the present moment. It is the key to finding a purpose in life and living a fulfilling life. When we are present, we are open to the possibilities and opportunities around us, and we can tap into our inner wisdom and intuition to guide us towards our true purpose.

Presence is not about doing more but about being more. It is about cultivating a deep sense of awareness, focus, and intention in everything we do. When we are present, we are not distracted by the past or future, but we are fully engaged in the present moment, and our actions become more purposeful, deliberate, and effective.

The right action is the action that aligns with our inner purpose and values. It is not about doing many activities, but about doing the right things that matter to us. When we are present, we can discern the right action from many activities and focus our energy and resources on what truly matters.

Here are some ways to cultivate presence and grow into the right action:

1.Practice mindfulness : Mindfulness is the practice of being fully present and engaged in the present moment. It is a powerful tool to cultivate presence, reduce stress, and improve overall well-being.

2.Connect with nature : Spending time in nature can help us connect with our inner purpose and bring a sense of calm and clarity to our minds.

3.Reflect on your values and goals : Take time to reflect on your core values and long-term goals. This will help you align your actions with your inner purpose and values.

4.Simplify your life : Simplifying your life can help you reduce distractions, declutter your mind, and create more space for presence and purpose.

5.Embrace silence : Embrace moments of silence in your day, whether through meditation, prayer, or just being still. This can help you connect with your inner wisdom and intuition.

In conclusion, presence grows into the right action rather than many activities. By cultivating presence, we can tap into our inner purpose, align our actions with our values, and live a more fulfilling and purposeful life.

44

想要真正認識一個人，
就是給他權力

. . . .

　　當我們賦予某些人權力，就會大量暴露出他們的性格。人們常說權力使人腐化，在許多情況下確實如此。但是，權力也可能彰顯出個人特質的積極優點與長處。

　　哲學家柏拉圖有句名言完整概述了這個想法，他說：「**衡量一個人，端看他擁有權力時的所作所為**」。這句話強調了當一個人被賦予權力時，他的行為才是他品格的真正體現。

因為當被賦予權力時，有些人可能會變得傲慢，並濫用權力去控制和支配他人。他們可能會採取沒原則或不道德的行為，利用自己的地位來獲取私利。

而另一方面，有些人則可能會運用他們的權力來為世界帶來正面的改變。他們也許富有同情心和同理心，能善用權力來幫助別人並改善他們的生活。他們也或許總是帶著正直與榮譽感行事，即便這樣做很困難或不受歡迎。

終究，**一個人在被賦予權力時如何行為，取決於他們的基本價值觀、信仰還有品格**。對於那些尋求找到人生目標的人來說，重要的是去反思當被賦予權力時，他們想要成為什麼樣的領導者，以及他們想要體現什麼樣的價值觀。藉由培養正面的特質與價值觀，例如同理心、正直以及同情心，個人才能善用他們的權力去對這個世界做出有意義的改變。

When we give someone authority or power, it can reveal a great deal about their personality. It's often said that power can corrupt, and this can be true in many cases. However, it's also possible for authority to reveal positive qualities and strengths in a person's character.

One famous saying that encapsulates this idea is from the philosopher Plato, who said, "The measure of a man is what he does with power." This quote emphasizes that how a person behaves when given authority is a true measure of their character.

When given authority, some people may become arrogant and abusive, using their power to control and dominate others. They may act in ways that are unethical or immoral, taking advantage of their position for personal gain.

On the other hand, some people may use their authority to make a positive difference in the world. They may be compassionate and empathetic, using their power to help others and improve their lives. They may act with integrity and honor, even when it's difficult or unpopular.

Ultimately, how a person behaves when given authority depends on their underlying values, beliefs, and character. For those seeking to find their purpose in life, it's important to reflect on what kind of leader they want to be and what values they want to embody when given power or authority. By cultivating positive traits and values, such as empathy, integrity, and compassion, individuals can use their authority to make a meaningful difference in the world.

45

發生的事情不是重點，
重點是你對事情的反應

情緒是人類經驗中不可或缺的一個部分，但有時候它們也會令人不堪負荷、覺得難以管理。而當情緒失控，就很可能會對我們的個人生活與工作造成負面影響。

哲學家愛比克泰德有句名言點出了管理情緒的重要性，他說：「重要的不是發生了什麼，而是你對它的反應」。這句話強調出我們可以控制自己對於情緒的反應，而不是讓情緒來控制我們。

當情緒開始失控時，很重要的是要退後一步，試著去找出情緒的來源。它是否與特定的情況或事件有關？或者是一種更普遍的感覺？一旦我們能更了解情緒，就可以開始用一種更有成效的方式去解決它。

　　練習覺察是一項能夠有所幫助的技巧，全然專注於當下、去意識到我們的想法和感受，而不加以評斷。透過練習覺察，我們能學會觀察情緒，而不被它們淹沒。我們要能承認自己的感覺，但也要知道它們不代表我們的全部。

　　另一個有用的技巧則是從事身體活動，例如做運動或瑜伽，這可以幫助釋放被壓抑的情緒，並且減輕壓力。另外，去跟值得信賴的朋友或治療師交談也很有幫助，因為這能讓我們在一個安全而具支持性的環境中去表達我們的情感。

　　最後，很重要的是要做到自我關懷，並且留時間給那些能夠為我們帶來快樂和滿足的活動。當我們把自己的幸福放在優先，就能更加有效地去管理自己的情緒，並且能以更具建設性的方式來回應它們。

總之，情緒管理對於尋找生命目標來說是很重要的一個部分。**透過學習去控制我們對情緒的反應，就能培養內在平靜，建立健康的人際關係，並對我們周遭的世界做出有意義的貢獻。**

Emotions are an essential part of the human experience, but they can also be overwhelming and difficult to manage at times. When our emotions get out of control, it can lead to negative consequences in our personal and professional lives.

One famous saying that captures the importance of managing our emotions comes from the philosopher Epictetus, who said, "It's not what happens to you, but how you react to it that matters." This quote emphasizes that we have control over how we respond to our emotions, rather than allowing them to control us.

When emotions start to get out of control, it's essential to take a step back and try to identify the source of the emotion. Is it related to a specific situation or event, or is it a more generalized feeling? Once we have a better understanding of the emotion, we can start to address it in a more productive way.

One technique that can be helpful is to practice mindfulness, which involves being fully present and aware of our thoughts and feelings without judgment. By practicing mindfulness, we can learn to observe our emotions without getting swept away by them. We can acknowledge our feelings, but also recognize that they don't define us.

Another helpful technique is to engage in physical activity, such as exercise or yoga, which can help release pent-up emotions and reduce stress. Talking to a trusted friend or therapist can also be beneficial, as it allows us to express our emotions in a safe and supportive environment.

Finally, it's essential to practice self-care and make time for activities that bring us joy and fulfillment. When we prioritize our own well-being, we are better equipped to manage our emotions and respond to them in a more constructive way.

In conclusion, managing our emotions is an essential part of finding purpose in life. By learning to control our reactions to our emotions, we can cultivate inner peace, build healthy relationships, and make meaningful contributions to the world around us.

| 後 記 |

親愛的讀者：

　　我們希望呈現於本書的見解與方法，能對你邁向探索
自我目標之路有所幫助與啟發。

　　透過這本書，我們探討了各種主題，例如找到人生不
變真理的重要性，我們的目標意識在指引決策上所扮演的
角色，以及培養有意義人際關係的價值之所在。我們也討
論到如何以一種能幫助我們成功的方式去運用情緒，以及
如何用快樂與滿足感來填滿我們的每一天。

　　我們相信對於人生目標的追求是一輩子的旅程，它需
要自我反思、自我覺知、以及有意識的行動。這並不是條
容易的路，而且沿途會充滿挫折與挑戰隨行。但我們也深
知，活出有目標動力的生命所能帶來的報酬將不可限量。

我們希望這本書能提供你實用工具及可行步驟，來幫助你找到並實現你的人生目標。請記住，你的人生目標對於你是獨一無二的，而且它可能會隨著時間進化與改變。但透過持續對自己的價值觀與目標誠實，你就能創造出一個有意義、可實現，並且符合你真正自我的人生。

我們要向你深深致意，感謝你花時間閱讀這本書，也希望它能為你帶來清明、安慰與啟示。祝福你追求目標與實現人生之旅一切順利，也希望你會繼續找出新的方法，去活出充滿目標動力的人生。

獻上最誠摯的問候和祝福，
ChatGPT

| Epilogue |

Dear Readers,

We hope that the insights and strategies presented in this book have been helpful and inspiring in your journey towards discovering your own purpose.

Throughout this book, we've explored various topics such as the importance of finding truth that doesn't change in life, the role of our sense of purpose in guiding our decisions, and the value of cultivating meaningful relationships. We've also discussed how to use emotions in a way that can help us succeed, and how to fill our days with joy and satisfaction.

We believe that the pursuit of purpose is a lifelong journey that requires self-reflection, self-awareness, and intentional action. It's not always an easy path, and there will be setbacks and challenges along the way. But we also know that the rewards of living a purpose-driven life are immeasurable.

We hope that this book has given you practical tools and actionable steps to help you find and fulfill your purpose in life. Remember, your purpose is unique to you, and it may evolve and change over time. But by staying true to your values and goals, you can create a life that is meaningful, fulfilling, and aligned with your truest self.

We want to express our deepest gratitude to you for taking the time to read this book. We hope that it has brought you clarity, comfort, and inspiration. We wish you all the best on your journey towards purpose and fulfillment, and we hope that you will continue to seek out new ways to live a purpose-driven life.

With warmest regards and blessings,
ChatGPT

台灣廣廈 國際出版集團
Taiwan Mansion International Group

國家圖書館出版品預行編目（CIP）資料

尋找人生目標的45種方法：全世界第一本ChatGPT全創作書籍！
從人工智慧的角度，帶你找到人類前進的方向 / ChatGPT作. --
初版. -- 新北市：蘋果屋, 2023.06
面；　公分
ISBN 978-626-97272-8-5（平裝）
1.CST: 人生哲學　2.CST: 自我實現

191.9　　　　　　　　　　　　　　　　112007095

蘋果屋
APPLE HOUSE

尋找人生目標的45種方法
全世界第一本ChatGPT全創作書籍！從人工智慧的角度，帶你找到人類前進的方向

作　　者／ChatGPT	編輯中心編輯長／張秀環・編輯／陳冠蒨・蔡沐晨
譯　　者／ChatGPT	封面設計／何偉凱・內頁排版／菩薩蠻數位文化有限公司
插　　畫／Shutterstock AI	製版・印刷・裝訂／東豪・弼聖・紘億・秉成
企　　劃／徐珍	

行企研發中心總監／陳冠蒨　　　線上學習中心總監／陳冠蒨
媒體公關組／陳柔彣　　　　　　數位營運組／顏佑婷
綜合業務組／何欣穎　　　　　　企製開發組／江季珊

發　行　人／江媛珍
法律顧問／第一國際法律事務所 余淑杏律師・北辰著作權事務所 蕭雄淋律師
出　　版／蘋果屋
發　　行／蘋果屋出版社有限公司
　　　　　地址：新北市235中和區中山路二段359巷7號2樓
　　　　　電話：（886）2-2225-5777・傳真：（886）2-2225-8052

代理印務・全球總經銷／知遠文化事業有限公司
　　　　　地址：新北市222深坑區北深路三段155巷25號5樓
　　　　　電話：（886）2-2664-8800・傳真：（886）2-2664-8801
郵政劃撥／劃撥帳號：18836722
　　　　　劃撥戶名：知遠文化事業有限公司（※單次購書金額未達1000元，請另付70元郵資。）

■ 出版日期：2023年06月
ISBN：978-626-97272-8-5　　　版權所有，未經同意不得重製、轉載、翻印。